The New Economic Landscape
in Europe

B

The New Economic Landscape in Europe

Horst Siebert

BLACKWELL
Oxford UK & Cambridge USA

Copyright © Horst Siebert 1991

Horst Siebert is hereby identified as author of this work in accordance with Section 77
of the Copyright, Designs and Patents Act 1988.

First published 1991

Basil Blackwell Ltd
108 Cowley Road, Oxford, OX4 1JF, UK

Basil Blackwell, Inc.
3 Cambridge Center
Cambridge, Massachusetts 02142, USA

Library of Congress Cataloging in Publication Data

Siebert, Horst, 1938–
The new economic landscape in Europe / Horst Siebert.
p.   cm.
Includes bibliographical references and index.
ISBN 0–631–18217–9
1. Europe—Economic integration.   2. Europe. Eastern—Economic
conditions—1989–   3. Germany—Economic conditions—1990–
I. Title.
HC241.S533   1991
330.94′0559—dc20   91–14339   CIP

British Library Cataloguing in Publication Data

A CIP catalogue record for this book is available from the British Library.

Typeset in 11 on 13 pt Ehrhardt
by Hope Services (Abingdon) Ltd.
Printed in Great Britain by T. J. Press Ltd., Padstow, Cornwall

This book is printed on acid-free paper.

Contents

List of Figures

List of Tables

Preface

The economic landscape of Europe is changing. In Western Europe, the single market has given new momentum to the European Community (EC), and the country-of-origin principle (see p. 4) and mutual recognition of national rules and regulations has started a process of institutional competition. National regulations will coexist, and arbitrage of consumers, firms and factors of production will lead to an *ex post* adjustment of national rules if necessary. Institutional competition can be interpreted as an exploratory device to find a more efficient institutional arrangement. Thus, the single market is an institutional innovation.

In Eastern Europe there is an even greater institutional innovation in the changing economic system. The central planning approach has proved to be completely inefficient and unable to provide enough goods for people. The economic system has to be changed from top to bottom. Decentralization through markets, including the market for corporate control, the introduction of property rights, establishment of hard currencies, opening up of the economies to participate in the international division of labour and real adjustment in firms will be major aspects of the metamorphosis of the planning system. The transformation of socialist economies is a major institutional change.

German integration can be analysed as a special case in the transformation of socialist economies. Of the three major areas of reform – establishment of the institutional infrastructure, monetary stabilization and real adjustment – the first two are already solved. Thus the German case can be considered as a laboratory experiment in which only the real adjustment problem is an issue.

The EC will have to open up to the Eastern European countries, and the European economic space of the future can be viewed as a system of rings. The EC is the core, with fully integrated commodity and capital markets. This core will be enlarged by a ring of European Free Trade Association (EFTA) countries, such as Austria, Sweden and Norway, joining the EC. Around the enlarged Community, there is another ring of countries associated with the EC through a free trade arrangement, such as Poland, Czechoslovakia and Hungary. Finally, there is a ring of countries that are less intensively integrated with the EC, such as the Baltic states, some regions of the USSR and possibly Russia itself.

In the new economic landscape of Europe, there is some concern that the EC will not be strong enough to have open markets with the world. As well as the protection already given to agriculture and ailing industries, there are new protectionistic tendencies, as in the Common Automobile Policy or industrial targeting. It would be ironic if the liberalization process in Eastern Europe discovered the merit of the free market while Western Europe moved in a protectionist direction.

The theme in this book is the institutional change in Western and Eastern Europe and its implications for the economic landscape in Europe. I developed this theme in a lecture series organized by VOSEKO, the Alumni Association at the Faculty of Economics of the Rijksuniversiteit Gent, where I held the Vereniging voor Economie-Chair during the winter term 1990–1. This series is sponsored every two years by the VVE, the Alumni Association of the Economics Faculties of the four Flemish universities of Antwerpen, Brussels, Gent and Leuven. I acknowledge the interest and critical comments of the students and the faculty at Gent, especially Professor M. De Clercq.

I have discussed the topics with researchers at the Kiel Institute of World Economics, especially institutional competition with Michael Koop. Bert Hofman and Michael Rauscher have criticized a first version of the whole text. Jens Schulte-Bockum has read the manuscript, and Lars Kumkar helped with the figures. Of course, many ideas floating around at the Institute have found their way into my writings. Finally, Jutta Arpe and Britta Eberleh have typed the many versions with excellent efficiency and great patience.

Horst Siebert

1

The Single Market – an Institutional Innovation

1.1 Reducing Market Segmentation

In the early 1980s the ghost of Eurosclerosis haunted Europe. The old continent, including the British Isles, seemed to be paralysed by regulations, somewhat crippled, like Laocoön entangled by the serpents of national regulations, market entry barriers and exit conditions, in recession with negative or low growth rates and losing jobs – for example, 0.8 million between 1973 and 1983 in the Federal Republic of Germany. The spirit of Joseph Schumpeter – the economist of economic development and change – had said farewell to Europe and moved to the USA and the Pacific Rim, to Japan and the four tigers.

Since 1985, the economic landscape of Europe has changed considerably, both in the west and in the east. It is now five years since an EC White Paper launched the project for the completion of the internal market. Three hundred steps were packaged and sold by Jacques Delors and Lord Cockfield and 'caught on'. The basic strategy is simple: abolish or reduce market segmentations that still exist, facilitate free market access, and establish the free movement of people, goods, services and factors of production, the so-called four freedoms. Will the single European market prove to be an institutional innovation, a Schumpeterian event in a region of the world that has been characterized by Eurosclerosis and over-regulation? Is Europe 1992 an example of political entrepreneurship in the sense of Schumpeter and will we see 'new combinations of means of production' (Schumpeter, 1934, p. 74)? Or is Europe a 'flash in the pan', *flambé à la* Delors, concocted by Cockfield, propagated by the press, public speeches and scientific conferences, but eventually dying from internal rent-seeking and protectionism?

Of the 300 directives, later reduced to 282, 158 had been adopted by the European Council by 28 March 1990, or a common position had been reached on them. Critics point out that some of these steps refer to such trivial points as the harmonization of statistics, or directives for eradication of contagious bovine pleuro pneumonia in Portugal and Spain and of blue tongue in the Greek isles. 'Implementation Directive 74/150/EEC' for tractors and agricultural machines specifies weight and dimensions, drive shaft, engine stopping device, windscreen wipers and foot rests. Or take 'Implementation Directive 87/402/EEC' from 25 June 1989, which is 'for rollover protection structures of tractors and agricultural machines incorporating two pillars mounted in front of the driver's seat on narrow-track wheeled agricultural and forestry tractors'. Other steps already taken are more important, however, relating, for example, to the liberalization of the capital market and the mutual recognition of university degrees. Still to come are decisions on such vital issues as the harmonization of the value added tax rates and a sweeping liberalization of transport services. In the Single European Act, unanimity in the Council of Ministers was replaced by majority voting (in a weighted form) for the larger part of the 282 directives. Unanimity is still required in the areas of taxation, free movement of labour and rights of employees. This procedural change has quickened implementation of the internal market programme.

It may be surprising that, despite pronouncements in the Treaty of Rome (1957) on the creation of a common market, Western Europe is still permeated by market segmentations. Where are they to be found? Market segmentations still prevail in the form of border controls, market entry barriers, to some extent in quota systems, such as national import quotas according to Article 115 on automobile imports, multifibre quotas and agricultural quotas, and in distortions caused by national subsidies.

Border controls exist for the collection of statistical information, because of differences in indirect taxation and for the enforcement of national regulations. Since value added tax is levied in the country of destination, reimbursement for intra-European exports requires the statistical monitoring of exports at the national border if tax rates differ as they do. For example, the value added tax rate is 14 per cent in Germany and 22 per cent in Denmark. For certain commodities, Belgium, France, Greece, Italy, Portugal and Spain have tax rates ranging from 28 to 38 per cent (table A1 in the appendix).

Barriers to market entry arise from differences in national regulations. Technical standards or product norms for consumer protection are cases in point, such as product norms for pharmaceutical products and hazardous material, licensing of new products in the chemical industry and environmental product standards.

Market entry conditions for firms result from licensing processes in land use planning, in activities with environmental impacts in regulated industries, in public procurement and in other regulated areas such as banking, insurance and the crafts. Entry barriers are influenced not only by the system defining entry *per se*, but also by national regulations on the conduct of business, such as the licensing of freight rates, insurance rates and conditions of the banking industry. Moreover, exit conditions influence entry. Barriers to market entry may also result from specific forms of property rights, as in common carrier problems (electricity). Finally, public procurement is a cause of an important entry barrier (postal services, tele-communications). These market entry barriers for firms represent the most severe market segmentations in Western Europe.

1.2 Institutional Competition versus Prior Harmonization

When the Common Market was established in 1958, the approach was to create a common European institutional setting by explicitly harmonizing the legal systems of all European countries. In the past two decades, this approach has given way to the realization that an *ex ante* harmonization on the European level is impractical.

The establishment of the single market in Europe raises the question of the extent to which Europe needs a uniform institutional arrangement in which private decisions take place. A basic issue is whether uniformity in the institutional arrangement is needed at all – whether institutional variety is not a merit *per se*, allowing national preferences to play. Besides this issue of the role of the subsidiary principle, or whether there should be a more centralized structure or a federal structure with some European skeleton law, the problem of institutional uniformity or variety relates to the time dimension of integration: does the single European market require *ex ante* harmonization of national policy instruments and of national institutional arrangements, or can harmonization be delegated to a competitive process between the institutional arrangements of European nations?

The strategies of *ex ante* and *ex post* harmonization have an important feedback to European integration. If *ex ante* harmonization is the appropriate approach, the institutional arrangements of the 12 EC countries have to be adjusted by a bargaining process in Brussels. If a competitive process is relied upon, harmonization will occur over time, and the solution will not have to be found immediately. Moreover, the extent of harmonization will be determined in a decentralized process of private decisions and national policy choices. Finally, *ex post* harmonization may not be total, leaving some differences in national institutional arrangements.

In 1979, the European Court of Justice handed down its Cassis-de-Dijon ruling. Cassis-de-Dijon or Crème-de-Cassis – an ingredient of Kir Royale or Kir Ordinaire – is a fruit liqueur that was forbidden in Germany because it had (and still has) an alcohol content of roughly 17 per cent whereas the German *Branntweinmonopolgesetz* of 1922 required a much higher alcohol content (32 per cent), supposedly to 'protect' the German consumer. According to the Cassis-de-Dijon ruling, a product legally brought to market in one country of the EC can automatically enter the markets of the other countries. Hence, Belgian beer can now be sold in Germany even if it is not brewed according to the German purity law of 1517. And German noodles (not made of hard wheat) can now be sold in the home of pasta (made of hard wheat). French pâté can compete with German leberwurst even if the former does not comply with German sausage regulations. This all results from the Cassis-de-Dijon decision made by the European Court. Thus, in the trade of products it is not the regulation of the country of destination but that of the country of origin that applies (the country-of-origin principle). With mutual recognition of the institutional arrangements of the country of origin, *ex ante* harmonization is not required.

The Commission is determined to extend the principle of mutual recognition to the service industries. A service allowed according to the rules of one country is allowed in other countries under the norms of the country of origin: UK insurance rates can be offered in Germany; Dutch freight rates apply for Dutch truckers doing business in Germany. Together with the liberalization of capital movement this may prove to be a tremendous stimulus to the service industries.

One of the major implications of the country-of-origin principle is that there will be institutional competition between national regulations. What does this mean? An important ingredient of the country-of-origin principle is the arbitrage of households and firms. With markets no longer being segmented, households and firms can take advantage of price differentials in the commodity and factor markets. Households will buy the commodity with the lower value added tax or they will shop in the country with the lower indirect tax rate. Trading houses, direct mailers and wholesalers will have scope for arbitrage between different countries.

Firms will exploit price and factor price differentials and differences in regulation. Location arbitrage will be a reaction to differences in production and business taxes, in market entry regulations, in environmental policy, in wage rates and labour market conditions and in prices of other immobile factors. Firms, or at least their sub-units, will migrate to the most favourable location. Location arbitrage results from the interplay of mobile and immobile factors of production and endowment. Immobile factors, including the institutional setting, determine the price of the mobile factors before arbitrage takes place and thus influence the attractiveness of a region or nation. After arbitrage, prices for mobile factors should be equal. Locational competition is the competition of the immobile factors for the mobile factor.

The arbitrage of consumers and firms will clearly reveal which national regulatory system is best in the eyes of the consumer or the producer: national regulation has to pass a litmus test of private agents voting with their purses and with their feet. Accordingly, there will be pressure on national regulations to adjust over time.

The competition approach to European integration is appealing for several reasons. First, harmonization is not undertaken *ex ante* at the political bargaining table under the influence of interest groups, rather it follows from an anonymous market process in which the power of interest groups evaporates. This relates to issues of taxation, product standards that can no longer be defended by a national interest group, and market entry conditions. Thus, no final piece of legislation has to be found beforehand, and various combinations of national regulations may exist at the same time. This seems to be especially relevant in an integrated market with fixed exchange rates. Without floating exchange rates, differences in legislation may be one of the few chances for the weaker economies to gain a comparative advantage. Greek companies paying Danish tax rates or Portuguese firms subject to a German social security system could be predicted to go bankrupt fairly quickly. Second, competition is an open-ended approach, the results of which are not known *ex ante*. Thus, institutional competition can be interpreted as an exploratory device in the sense of Hayek (1968). It is profitable for countries to imitate successful legislation or to try to come up with new laws when unsatisfactory results have been achieved. Third, harmonizing the national laws from above, which was attempted in the 1950s, 1960s and 1970s, has proved impractical. Fourth, the principle of mutual recognition is a mechanism to break up national regulations that become embedded in the national political process. Institutional competition can be viewed as an innovation for reducing institutional rigidities and the power of vested interests, especially if it relates to national regulations that define entry and exit conditions on goods and factor markets. This seems to be the most important application of institutional competition in the European setting. The Cassis-de-Dijon ruling of the European Court of Justice is the major case in point. The establishment of the country-of-origin-principle introduced the principle of mutual recognition. Fifth, institutional competition reveals the opportunity costs of national regulation when those who are affected move out of the area of regulation. Thus, if exit from national regulations is possible, the opportunity costs will become apparent, and this is an important aspect in determining the optimal level of national regulation. In this interpretation institutional competition may be instrumental in the taming of Leviathan (S. Sinn, 1990). Last, but not least, institutional competition keeps Western Europe flexible enough to let new countries enter the EC. Institutional competition is consistent with an open club.

The conflict between the integration strategy of institutional competition and prior harmonization reflects a more fundamental conflict of orientation in Europe. On a constitutional level, this discord is concerned with the manner of organizing a society in terms of institutions, it is the conflict of federalism with centralization. On a philosophical level, it is the clash between liberalism in the European sense and a more planning-oriented approach. We have diverging views in Europe on such issues as confidence in the functioning of markets versus some type of control and interventionism, sovereignty of the consumer versus the need for his or her 'protection', the role and the size of government, spontaneity of autonomous decision-making and decentralized processes versus a constructionism, or English case law versus the logic of the Roman law. Europe is in a process of searching for its institutions, and the showdown between the British and the French concepts of Europe is still to come.

1.3 The Economic Impact

The country-of-origin principle will make market entry easier, and markets will become more contestable. Entry is an important prerequisite for the contestability of markets. If entry is possible, the firm already established is restrained in its price setting behaviour: high prices and high profits attract the newcomer. Thus the threat of market entry will reduce prices and rents. Access to a restricted market can be interpreted as a property right; a change in market access is a change in the property right and in the rent associated with it. Freer market access will be especially relevant for those sectors that are heavily regulated. This holds true for important service sectors and public procurement.

1 Banks will have easier access to the market in other countries and can take advantage of differences in national regulations. Bank customers can use the services of a bank in a foreign country because of the liberalization of capital flows. This may include access to new financial products for the customer. Moreover, investment banks may enter the market of the more traditional universal bank.

2 In insurance, the principle of mutual recognition will allow the regulation of the country of origin to apply. The British insurance company can offer insurance rates licensed in Great Britain anywhere in Europe. Insurance companies and banks are becoming strong competitors in attracting loanable funds and allocating them to competing users.

3 In road freight, free market access would imply the removal of cabotage rules for the foreign driver; existing licences, which are

property rights because of restricted entry, would lose (part of) their value, and competition would be intensified with this type of deregulation – reductions in transportation costs of 30 per cent in Germany are expected. With such cost reductions, the relative competitive position of other means of transportation will be affected, implying a loss in market volume for the railways. Issues such as financing the transportation infrastructure (roads), treating railways and roads in an equivalent fashion and internalizing the environmental effects of road transport will have to be solved.[1]

4 In the airline industry, free market entry implies that routes in Europe will no longer be licensed bilaterally to the respective national airlines but to other competitors as well. Allocating landing slots with a price mechanism is another important step. Again, a change in property rights will influence the intensity of competition.

5 In the electricity industry, free market entry can be established if a new property right for the common carrier is defined. For instance, the French energy utilities are interested in supplying energy across their national borders. Germany's 'century contract', securing the coal industry's sales to the electricity sector, is rightly being questioned.

6 Postal and telecommunication services – which are close substitutes – have been supplied by state-owned companies in most countries since the nineteenth century. Splitting up these services and privatizing them, or at least some functions, is a precondition for opening these markets.

7 In public procurement, institutional arrangements and actual practices favour a generous use of public funds because there is neither control by competition nor allocation of funds by market principles.

In all these areas, depending on how fully free market entry is introduced, we can expect an increase in the contestability of markets.

Other factors also point in the direction of more contestable markets. The size of the Western European market, with 340 million people, will change the economic environment of firms. To the extent that the large internal market is not already being tapped, there will be

---

[1] Solutions include user charges for roads and splitting railways, into one company owning the infrastructure and many operating companies, possibly private.

falling average costs, at least for a certain range of output. In production, firms will move down the average cost curve by allocating high fixed costs to a larger number of units. At the same time there will be learning effects in the accumulation of experience. Such so-called dynamic effects occur in activities with highly qualified labour (electronics, aerospace products). For multi-product firms, spin-offs from one product to the other may be relevant. Moreover, there are economies of scale in research and development. Economies of scale hold not only for production but also for marketing, such as in establishing a Europe-wide brand name, and for distribution. They also relate to some services, such as insurance because of risk spreading, and banking because of the fixed costs of headquarter services, which can be apportioned to a larger number of transactions.

The argument of falling average cost curves applies to quite a few sectors, namely aircraft production and other transport equipment (e.g. the automobile industry), the chemical industry, man-made fibres and paper, printing and publishing, the pharmaceutical industry and biochemical products. Table 1.1 shows empirical estimates of falling average costs for selected sectors in manufacturing. Economies of scale are measured by halving the minimum efficient technical scale (METS), which is defined as the scale at which unit costs cease to fall. Halving the minimum efficient costs, i.e. halving the size of the firm, will lead to an increase in costs. This cost increase is the measure of the economies of scale.

The extent to which potential economies of scale can be realized depends on the size of the market and on the preferences of the consumer for the firm's product. Here we observe two different trends in Europe. On the one hand we can expect that demand (and preferences?) will become more similar throughout Europe because living conditions and income per head will level to some extent. This trend makes for a larger market and more economies of scale. On the other hand, there is a demand for more variety with higher income, a demand for choice between a Peugeot and a Fiat, and this wish for product differentiation will operate to create market niches for individual firms. The net effect is open. However, the role of economies of scale is reduced if consumers want variety and thus limit the size of the market that a product can catch. Another factor influencing the realization of economies of scale is organizational costs, which may represent a brake on falling average costs and may

Table 1.1 Branches of manufacturing industry ranked by size of economies of scale

Branch	Cost gradient at half METS (per cent)
Motor vehicles	6–9
Other means of transport	8–20
Chemical industry	2.5–15
Man-made fibres	5–10
Metals	≥6
Office machinery	3–6
Mechanical engineering	3–10
Electrical engineering	5–15
Instrument engineering	5–15
Paper, printing and publishing	8–36
Non-metallic mineral products	≥6
Metal articles	5–10 (castings)
Rubber and plastics	3–6
Drink and tobacco	1–6
Food	3.5–21
Other manufacturing	n.a.
Textile industry	10 (carpets)
Timber and wood	n.a.
Footwear and clothing	1 (footwear)
Leather and leather goods	n.a. 18

n.a.: not available.
Source: Emerson et al., 1988, table 6.1.1

eventually cause average costs to rise. Dynamic gains of integration are not only due to the static exploitation of economies of scale. Intensified competition, that is the contestability of markets, is the main driving force for innovation and a more efficient allocation; and we can expect that the single market will intensify competition.

Consequently, the role of economies of scale should not be overestimated.

In the realm of high fixed costs and falling average costs, life for the small firm is not easy. The small firm has to find a market niche that the large firm will not enter, or has not entered, it has to produce a new or better product, or a specialized product, and it has to use a more innovative production process. Fortunately, smaller firms tend to be more flexible and to have better contacts with their customers. Their potential will also be enhanced when large firms are of the dinosaur-type. Small and middle-sized firms can be a vigorous force for innovation, and Europe would be well advised not to favour the 'super corporations' or become a 'Europe Incorporated'. Empirical evidence from the United States suggests that small firms, with 20 or fewer employees, created almost two-thirds of the net new jobs in the USA (Birch, 1984). In the western part of Germany, 78 per cent of all jobs in manufacturing (*gewerbliche Wirtschaft*) are provided by firms with less than 500 employees (Schmidt, 1990). Moreover, the potential to exploit economies of scale is limited by the market segment a firm can conquer. This in turn depends on product quality as perceived by the consumer. Consequently, the relevance of economies of scale is limited.

Besides free market access, the size of the market and economies of scale, there is an increased potential for cost minimization and location arbitrage of firms. Thus we can observe relocation of firms or the establishment of new branches of firms in Europe, especially in Spain. The spatial restructuring of firms is an intra-firm realization of comparative advantages. It goes hand in hand with an increased mobility of capital.

Expectations of firms also play a role, and the expectations of the business community seem to be positive with respect to the single market. An observable reaction is the organizational restructuring of industry and the service sector, for instance the definition of new firm strategies for the single market or the establishment of new forms of cooperation between firms supplying separate national markets (because of only nationally established brand names). Mergers and acquisitions are vehicles by which a firm can establish itself in the market of another country and streamline its product mix. According to a report of the European Commission, there were 184 mergers between firms from different members of the community in 1986/87,

The Single Market

424 in 1987/88 and 641 in 1988/89. In Germany, mergers have exploded from 34 in 1973 to 635 in 1980 and 1500 in 1990 (table A2).

As a long-run trend, investment in Europe relative to that in North America, Japan and the four tigers (South Korea, Hong Kong, Singapore and Taiwan) has declined. In figure 1.1, the relative performance of the EC, North America (USA and Canada) and Japan plus the four tigers with respect to locational investment is illustrated.[2] The position of the EC, which had been declining over

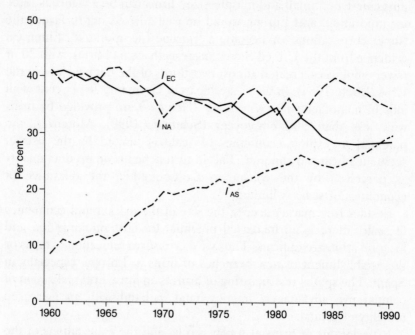

Figure 1.1 Locational investment in regions of the world
(percentage share).

Locational investment is defined as in footnote 2. I_{EC}, investment in the European Community; I_{NA}, investment in the USA and Canada; I_{AS}, investment in Japan, South Korea, Hong Kong, Singapore and Taiwan.

[2] Locational investment is defined as a fraction of investment in each of the three country groups in relation to total investment in all industrialized countries (S. Sinn, 1989b). Changes in this indicator may serve as a measure of a location's attractiveness for internationally mobile capital. The group of industrialized countries comprises all OECD countries plus the four tigers. Investment is defined as real gross domestic investment in international dollars at constant purchasing power parities and at

time, has been stable since 1985. Locational investment in North America, which during the 1960s and 1970s moved into line with the EC, increased considerably during the first half of the 1980s. This trend was reversed in 1986 and since then locational investment in North America has been converging towards the European level.

Foreign direct investment in Europe has increased. The stock of US direct investment in the EC went up from US$ 80.8 billion (1980) to US$ 136.7 billion in 1989. The stock of Japanese direct investment went up from US$ 7.1 billion (1983) to US$ 29.2 billion (1988). Canadian and Swedish direct investment has also increased. Within the EC, the UK, Spain and Portugal succeeded in attracting the largest share of direct investment.

1.4 A Caveat

There is undoubtedly a strong potential for Western Europe to become a Schumpeterian event, an institutional innovation. The reduction of internal trade barriers may not prove to be too important, since in commodity trade most obstacles – except border controls – have already been eliminated. The reduction of internal trade barriers will only be important in those areas where individual countries have used various non-tariff barriers to protect certain industries. A much greater stimulus will come from free market access in regulated sectors, especially in services, from more contestable markets and from mutual recognition of national regulations and institutional competition. This competitive process, pitting the various national regulations against each other, will result in the extinction of the least efficient and hence a crumbling of the power of the vested interests that generated their existence; it will imply a true liberalization of the European economies.

There are, of course, internal forces that may restrain the stimulus. One such force is the centralization of European regulations – call it a Brusselization. *Ex ante* harmonization does not take advantage of institutional competition; in many cases it will create inefficiencies, weaken the dynamic gains from institutional competition and lead to

------

constant national prices. Data for 1960–85 have been calculated from Summers and Heston (1988), those for 1986–90 are an estimate based on Summers and Heston's 1985 values and on growth rates of real gross capital formation.

internal rent-seeking. Another force is the attempt to evade intensified internal competition by reducing market access of non-member countries through protectionist trade policies.

Needless to say, the overall outcome for the world economy not only depends on Europe's trade policies but also on the behaviour of the other major trading partners. The experience of the 1930s suggests that the world would be better off by preventing regionalism and strategically oriented behaviour by individual nations or regional blocks. If Europe's Schumpeterian event is to be more than just a one night stand, if it can really play in Peoria, then the key lies in the door to the world economy – with mutual recognition inside and a most-favoured nation clause as well as a world market openness outside.

2

Institutional Competition

2.1 The Concept of Institutional Competition

The idea of competition between national jurisdictions goes back to the seminal work of Tiebout (1956), who examined the competition of communities. The decentralization of political decisions or the federal structure of government (Frey, 1977), more specifically fiscal federalism (McLure, 1983), regulatory federalism and fiscal equivalence (Olson, 1969) are important issues in this context. Recently, the approach of institutional competition has been used by the Kiel Institute of World Economics (Giersch, 1990; S. Sinn, 1989a, 1990; Siebert, 1989b; Siebert and Koop, 1990) and applied to various policy matters, such as environmental policy (Siebert, 1990a; Long and Siebert, 1991) and regional policy (Soltwedel, 1987).

In economic theory, the process and outcome of competition are well defined for factor and goods markets. Is there also a market for institutions and can the concept of competition be applied to it? The good traded in this market is a composite commodity, comprising regulations, institutional arrangements, taxation and government activities, such as the provision of public goods. On the supply side of the market governments can be identified. Federal, state and even local governments, as well as self-regulating institutions, are the suppliers of relevant legislation. Private households and firms constitute the demand side. In the context here, legislation is interpreted as a country-specific, immobile factor of production just like land or the environment.

Given this description, how does the market for institutions work? Governments can be thought of as maximizing the probability of being re-elected, with their objective function representing some aggregate of individual utility functions. They offer the whole range of regulations, activities and institutions of which the good 'institutional arrangement' consists. The variables of the utility functions of individuals are privately produced consumption goods and public goods. To simplify the analysis let us assume that only central governments exist and that these governments collect a tax, for instance per unit of capital employed in the production process. With the tax receipts, a public good is financed that can be used for consumption as well as for production, e.g. infrastructure, education and environmental quality. The public good may also be interpreted as the set of institutional arrangements that assure a certain quantity or quality of the public good being produced by private decisions. The tax rate is set so as to equate the marginal utility of the public good and the marginal utility of the private good. The marginal utility of using a unit of a resource in the production of the private good denotes the opportunity costs of the public good. Owners of financial capital and firms are assumed to maximize profits whereas households and workers are utility maximizers.

An important ingredient of the concept of institutional competition is the distinction between mobile and immobile factors of production. Land, environmental endowment and some types of labour, especially unskilled labour, are immobile. Capital is highly mobile before it is put in place (*ex ante*). Even if it is put in place, capital is mobile *ex post* according to the putty-clay model in the sense that depreciated capital might not be replaced. Admittedly, this type of capital mobility takes time.

With respect to the mobility of technical knowledge, different aspects have to be distinguished. As far as technical knowledge is embodied in labour, such as skills of craftsmen or capabilities of managers, the mobility of technical knowledge depends on the mobility of people. Information on new production technologies or new products, i.e. blueprint technical knowledge, is mobile in principle but its mobility depends on institutional arrangements, such as the patent system, property rights defining the transferability of knowledge and the spatial size of the owner (multinational firms). Basic knowledge tends to be more mobile than applied knowledge. Over time technical knowledge will diffuse, for instance with new suppliers (countries) moving through the product cycle.

When making their decisions on locations, internationally mobile factors evaluate the legislation offered by governments in terms of their maximization problem. In order to take advantage of legislation, the mobile factor has to be located in or at least relocated to the country in which this legislation is offered. Of course, the decision to move to another jurisdiction is made taking other relocation-related costs into account as well.

Institutional competition is the competition of immobile factors for mobile factors. Governments try to attract internationally mobile factors from abroad. Thus, competition for the mobile factor is one way of acquiring a comparative advantage. The inflow of factors of production generates an additional income for the immobile factor. For instance, the inflow of capital raises the marginal productivity of labour and should therefore make higher wages possible. From a dynamic perspective an increased marginal productivity of capital owing to a better allocation would induce additional investment. These positive effects of attracting mobile factors are the major incentive for all governments to invent better legislation and to influence their acquired comparative advantage. Of course, the most striking example of institutional competition is the exit of East Germans to the Federal Republic of Germany in 1989 and in the first three months of 1990. When mobile factors emigrate, they put a burden on the country of origin by reducing the income of immobile factors. Thus, governments have an incentive to adjust laws and regulations to the needs of firms and households. Adjusted regulations may then be again attractive to other factors and factor relocation to this country may occur.

In a wider interpretation, governments might provide not only pure public goods but also merit goods, relating to policy issues, such as consumer protection and social stability. These merit goods are supplied by regulations. The optimal national regulation equalizes the marginal benefits and the marginal costs of regulation, where the marginal benefits derive from an additional unit of the merit good. In this case, marginal opportunity costs do not arise from taxation of private activities but from restraint of the use of resources in the private sector. Institutional competition may be interpreted as providing better information on the opportunity costs of regulation and breaking deadlocks of regulations established by national pressure groups. Institutional competition, then, is a device to reduce the political power of interest groups, i.e. to reduce rent-seeking in a society and to correct a policy failure. It is an instrument to limit the manoeuvring space of rent-seekers and thus to reduce the strategic capabilities of firms *vis-à-vis* governments.

The crucial point of competition is that the supply side faces incentives to get involved in innovative activities; in the goods markets, these incentives are temporary monopoly profits. The major welfare-increasing effect of innovation, however, stems from the monopoly profits being competed down and from dissipation of the innovation in the market process. In the goods market, monopoly profits will eventually be eroded by competition among firms. Nevertheless, temporary profits represent an incentive for further research and innovation. On the market for legislation or other institutional arrangements, the positive effects for a country generated by the attraction of mobile resources can be interpreted as the country's temporary monopoly profits. Although there are no patents for legislation, the advantage of offering an improved type of legislation first can be quite valuable. This is especially true when the other countries' direct costs of imitation are high because of political obstacles.

Exit of factors of production is an important ingredient of institutional competition. A high degree of factor mobility is one of the major prerequisites for institutional arbitrage to produce an efficient solution. In a series of articles (e.g. Feldstein and Horioka, 1980; Obstfeld, 1986) attempts were made to measure the degree of international capital mobility. The results were extremely ambiguous, but in a comprehensive study for the EC Frankel (1989) found that capital mobility was almost perfect, with the negligible exceptions of Ireland and Greece. EC direct investment in other EC countries ranged from 15.4 per cent in the United Kingdom to as much as 54.7 per cent of total inward investment in France, where more than one out of two francs came from the EC (table A3 in the appendix).

In contrast to capital, labour mobility seems to be extremely low. In the six countries of the original EEC the stock of immigrants from other members of the EC of 12 amounted to only 0.45 per cent of the whole EC population. Although there are no major restrictions on where citizens of EC countries are allowed to settle down, specific regulations of the labour markets and the social security systems seem effectively to limit labour mobility. This is also true for qualified labour. Various kinds of educational prerequisites bar foreign applicants from obtaining jobs abroad and thus from relocation. It can, however, be expected that the liberalization of the EC's service sector will increase the mobility of qualified labour. In addition, technical know-how is considered to be increasingly mobile internationally, especially if it is bound to multinational corporations. Nevertheless, capital seems to be the major force that can effect arbitrage between national regulations.

Besides the mobility of people, both as residents and workers, and the mobility of capital, the mobility of the consumer and the mobility of commodities are important prerequisites for arbitrage in the goods markets. If people are mobile, they can buy where a good has the lowest price. And, of course, it is important that goods can be brought to the people.

2.2 Levelling the Playing Field?

Firms argue that they need a level playing field and they often complain about legislation-induced cost differentials between EC members. It is argued that once border controls are abolished and market segmentations are significantly reduced, firms in some countries face a comparative cost disadvantage because of different legislation. Since this disadvantage is not related to the firms' productivity and efficiency *per se* they claim that they are harmed by unfair competition. Therefore, a levelling of the playing field is requested, i.e. that regulations that directly alter costs or prices be harmonized. For instance, business taxes or the government-imposed costs of employing labour, such as social security contributions, lay-off constraints, etc., differ between countries.

Most prominent is the demand for harmonization of value added tax rates (VAT). The point made is that without harmonization firms in high tax countries will suffer from tax differentials, and the international division of labour will not be determined by comparative cost advantage but by comparative tax advantage. However, value added tax rates ranging from 2.1 to 38 per cent will open up almost unlimited opportunities for arbitrage once border controls are abolished. Shopping tourism and mail-order firms could flourish by taking advantage of tax-induced price differentials. In regions near a border even non-tradeables might be subject to arbitrage. A reduction in tax revenues and political pressure from firms negatively affected would force governments to lower tax rates. On the other hand, countries with relatively low rates might raise their rates. In the long run the gap between high and low rates can be expected to be narrowed by institutional competition, and *ex ante* harmonization is unnecessary.

Even if it is believed that the adjustment process of institutional competition would work too slowly in the case of value added taxes, there are other ways of coping with the problem. One is to harmonize VAT rates. Since value added taxes basically serve the purpose of financing government activities, this option was vetoed by high tax countries, which would have lost a considerable amount of tax revenue all at once. Another approach has been adopted by the EC Commission, which leaves different national rates unchanged. Domestic importers invoice the foreign VAT in the home country and then pay the domestic VAT rate. An EC clearing institution has to redistribute the tax revenues.

The harmonization of tax rates and the bureaucratic solution of the European Commission could be avoided by a re-alignment of exchange rates (Siebert, 1989c). The value added tax would be levied according to the country-of-origin principle at the domestic rate. The exchange rate change would just offset the differences in VAT rates and the price of imports would not change. The structure of VAT, the system of reduced and higher rates on certain goods, could be left to institutional competition.

2.3 The Problem of 'Zero-regulation'

Critics of the competition approach argue that the exit mechanism for mobile factors forces countries to adjust their levels of regulation in response to other countries that start to lower their levels of regulation. Once other countries have adjusted their legislation, the first country may start to relax its regulations further. In the end, this tendency would lead to a sub-optimal level of legislation and, in the extreme, to a state of zero-regulation. On the other hand, a lax regulation policy may imply too low a level of government activities, including the supply of public goods. Is this a problem of destructive competition, which creates a need for harmonization of national legislation?

This reasoning has been applied to a number of policy fields. In the tax competition debate it was claimed that the US tax cuts of the 1980s forced European governments to lower their tax rates as well in order to restore the competitiveness of their countries. In the EC, the argument goes, much lower relocation and other transactions costs would put even greater pressure on high tax countries to adjust their tax rates. In the final stage, the EC could look like a 'single' (large) tax haven (Giovannini and Hines, 1990, p. 1). At first sight, some evidence seems to support these arguments. Take, for instance, corporate income tax rates. In the mid-seventies the EC's average rate was approximately 47.21 per cent, with national rates ranging from 25 to as much as 56 per cent (table A4 of the appendix). Up to 1989, all EC members cut their tax rates, with the exception of Denmark and Italy. The EC's average tax rate went down to 42.33 per cent. Similar synchronous developments can also be recognized in the deregulation of financial markets and of the airline and telecommunication industries, and in the privatization of state-owned firms.

Firms decide on where to locate their capital by equating their net marginal rates of return in all countries. When the countries compete, one government may try to gain an advantage by lowering the tax rate per unit of profit. Since this government offers a higher net-of-tax return on physical capital, it attracts additional capital from abroad. Could this tax cut be the starting shot in a continuous process of lowering capital income taxes?

Lower tax rates have a two-fold effect. On the one hand, a reduction in taxes and increase in profits will stimulate investment and enlarge the capital stock, and this will lead to a higher production of the private good. On the other hand, it is argued that lower taxes may reduce revenues and, consequently, the level of infrastructure provided. If infrastructure is an input to the production process, the productivity of firms is negatively affected. In addition, a lower level of public goods directly makes consumers worse off. The competitive process balances these counteracting effects. In equilibrium the net welfare effect of a marginal tax cut is zero. Therefore, we observe a pressure on governments to use tax revenues efficiently to provide public goods. There is, however, no tendency to reach a tax rate of or close to zero. Clearly, the reason for this is the existence of opportunity costs of a low tax rate policy.

The argument that zero-regulation will not come about rests on the assumption that the user of the good provided by the government is the taxpayer (and the voter). Under this condition, goods are financed by benefit taxation with marginal benefits and marginal costs being equal for the user of and the payer for the good. The public good is transformed into a club good. This approach can be extended to the concept of fiscal equivalence (Olson, 1969), which implies appropriate property rights that internalize (and privatize) the costs of a public good. The members of a club enjoy the club good and contribute to its financing. For instance, user charges may be applied when firms employ the physical infrastructure (airports, roads) in the production process. In some areas, it would be optimal to finance some of these goods privately, for example in the communication industry. In transportation, more use could be made of private provision and of private financing of 'public' goods.

The hypothesis that institutional competition will not result in zero-regulation seems to break down if the users and the payers are different groups. However, in many cases there are links between the user and the payer. For instance, firms benefit from vocational training, university education and basic research, and would therefore be willing to pay capital income taxes. Note that labour also benefits from these government activities. The cultural infrastructure (museums, theatres etc.) is an important location factor for firms because it is instrumental in attracting qualified workers and management.

Another area in which the zero-regulation issue is discussed is the so-called 'social dimension' of the Common Market. 'Social dumping' and 'the death of the welfare state' are the catchwords in this debate. What is meant is that factor mobility may effectively limit redistribution. Net payers of redistribution would emigrate to countries with a rudimentary social security system, whereas net receivers of redistribution would gather in countries that offered a high degree of income redistribution. Clearly, the country of net receivers would be headed for bankruptcy. But even in the financing of the social security system, there are opportunity costs of reducing regulation. Admittedly, the link between the user and the payer may be weak from the firm's point of view, but it still exists. Improved social security can lower the riskiness of investment and increase labour productivity because of fewer sick-leaves, less strikes or better motivation of the labour force (Paqué, 1989). Since these factors increase the return on capital, firms are willing to pay contributions to the system of social security. These payments can be interpreted as user charges for the factor of social stability. The possibility of raising funds from capital for income redistribution, however, seems to be effectively limited. In open economies the scope for redistribution from mobile factors to immobile ones is small. This is little more than saying that governments cannot tax a good with a high price elasticity too much. This might be a reason to complain, but it is certainly not a reason to harmonize social security. Even if the EC were to do so, capital would leave the EC and nothing would be gained.

2.4 Competition and Currencies

An intellectually fascinating problem is whether institutional competition can be applied to the institutional arrangement for currencies. National monies would be mutually recognized as means of payment and would then compete against each other. Individual preferences could play. Currency substitution is yet another example of arbitrage by individual agents. In the long run, the national currency that is accepted by individuals will win (Hayek, 1977; Vaubel, 1978).

For political reasons it may not be acceptable for a national currency to be driven out by another national currency. Alternatively, one may attempt to create an artificial European currency unit, such as the ECU, and make it harder over time, hoping that it may drive out all the national currencies. This, however, requires that the basket concept be given up and that harder currencies get increased weight. In such a scenario, the ECU can get harder over time, but it can only get as hard as the hardest national currency at the limit. And the hardest currency is still around. Consequently, hardening the ECU by mimicking the currency substitution of the market does not provide a new anchor. There is still a need for the hard currency as the foundation stone of the monetary system.

Competition among currencies has the advantage of allowing realignments. Changes in the exchange rate alleviate structural problems among European countries by allowing depreciation for countries with a weaker competitiveness, thus serving as a shock absorber. In this respect, a re-alignment abates the political demand to reduce developmental or structural imbalances between European regions. A re-alignment would also reduce the role of a transfer mechanism. This becomes evident when we consider irrevocably fixed exchange rates. Assume labour to be immobile and assume that the conditions of the labour markets are harmonized throughout Europe, for instance with respect to wages. Then structural balance-of-payments and unemployment problems will arise, and there will be pressure for a political transfer mechanism. Apparently, institutional competition and re-alignment are interlinked. Re-alignments represent a substitute for harmonization in the real sector of the economy.

2.5 Diversity or Homogeneity of National Preferences?

The idea of currency substitution or the proposals for a European Monetary System point to an important aspect of the harmonization issue. What is the role of the preferences of individuals in the different nations? If individuals in the European countries have similar preferences, if their rankings of goods, economic conditions such as public infrastructure versus private goods, environmental quality, consumer protection, unemployment and inflation are identical, harmonization will not be too much of an issue. Under such a condition of homogeneity of preferences, individuals will apply the same ranking everywhere, and *de facto* conditions can only differ if the restraints to the optimization process in the countries vary. This is implied by the fact that *de facto* values of economic variables that are the result of individual optimization processes are derived from the ranking rules of individuals or firms and the economic constraints of the agents. For instance, when all Europeans value environmental quality relative to other goods in the same way, the *de facto* environmental conditions will only differ between countries when an identical ranking yields less weight for the environment in some countries because income per head is low, as in the periphery of the EC. In this case, a *de facto* adjustment in environmental quality will come about in the process of economic development. Income per head rising in the periphery will eventually give more weight to environmental quality, and *de facto* harmonization will come about *ex post*.

The harmonization issue becomes interesting when the preferences of individuals in different countries, as expressed in the political processes defining institutional arrangements, differ. Then the issue of harmonization becomes one of the extent to which differences in preferences, in short in national preferences, should be allowed to play. Do we need the same preferences with respect to obedience to a traffic light turning red in an ebullient Neapolitan as in a composed, rule-conscious car driver from Kiel? And is it necessary to have homogeneity of opinion on safety standards for lifts in Lisbon and in Aberdeen? The answer must be that national preferences should be allowed to play. We do not need a *Homo europaeus* or a *Homunculus brusseliensis*, with identical preference schedules from Hammerfest to Hiraklion. This implies that a federal structure and a process of institutional competition have the advantage of allowing differences in tastes.

If there are differences in national preferences on important issues, for instance on inflation, this clearly has implications for the approach to harmonization. Currency competition is one institutional answer to the problem of harmonization if national political preferences on inflation differ. When currency competition is ruled out for political reasons, any other institutional arrangement must ensure that price level stability can be obtained. Starting from the premise that preferences on this issue will continue to differ in Europe, a monetary institutional arrangement not relying on currency competition requires that national preferences accepting inflation cannot play. The controlling vigour of currency competition must now be embodied in the institutional arrangement of the monetary sector. In this context, it can be clearly seen that *ex ante* harmonization requires that national preferences are cut off to some extent.

Note that the lower inflation rates in some European countries, such as France in recent years, do not necessarily confirm a change in preferences but may be the result of restraints. In the European Monetary System, with an important central bank aiming at price level stability, the stabilization policy of countries is restrained by the interplay of purchasing power parity and interest rate parity. For a country allowing a high inflation rate, purchasing power parity will stimulate expectations that the currency will be depreciated; if such expectations are formed, capital will leave the country unless, according to interest rate parity, the interest rate rises. This, however, crowds out investment. Thus, the opportunity costs of higher interest rates and the risk of revealing the weakness of its currency to the electorate by depreciation force the inflation-prone country to expand its money supply in line with the money supply of the anchor. Observed low inflation rates may thus very well be the restraints of the institutional system.

Clearly diversity in national or regional preferences raises the issue of the institutional mechanism by which preferences should be aggregated in Europe. As in any national market economy, the basic mechanism for revealing preferences, and for aggregating them to the total willingness of a country to pay for the total output of a sector, is the market. For public goods, the political mechanism has to be relied upon. Again, a federal structure in the aggregation process in Europe should be relied upon, allowing decentralized preferences to play. Europe should follow the concept of fiscal equivalence, placing the provision and the funding of public goods at the most efficient level. What can best be done at the lowest level should be done there, according to the subsidiary principle and according to the idea of institutional competition.

2.6 Market Failure – a Justification for Harmonization?

Are there limits to the principle of institutional competition? The hypothesis that markets are efficient depends on a number of assumptions, which according to the supporters of the harmonization solution are not fulfilled on the EC's market for legislation. These unfulfilled factors are the standard reasons given for the emergence of market failure. Market failure and, consequently, an inferior allocation of resources are mainly caused by the existence of externalities and by strategic behaviour made possible by monopolistic or monopsonistic positions resulting from restrictions to market entry and exit. However, keeping the optimality of the perfect competition solution in mind, it is worth examining whether mechanisms for fixing market failure can be found without harmonization.

Externalities

The standard qualification of the perfect competition framework is that there are externalities. Technological externalities, as opposed to pecuniary externalities, occur when one country directly affects the variables of the production or utility functions of other countries, not through markets but through technological systems. The incurred costs or benefits are not taken into consideration by the originating country and no compensation is paid. In our context of a competitive process between national institutional arrangements, international externalities are relevant. Therefore, technological externalities among countries cause national legislation that yields Pareto-inferior results.

The issue is exemplified by the case of environmental policy, a field in which technological externalities often originate and where the economic decisions of individual agents, such as households and firms, in one country are technologically linked via the environment to agents in another country. In the case of cross-border pollution, the technological system consists of environmental media, such as air systems and rivers (see below). Another example is a contagious disease that may spread from one country to the other. Yet another example of technological externalities are 'bank runs', in which a bank in one country that goes bankrupt has an effect on banks in another country. As in the case of international pollution spill-overs, the institutional arrangements for these sectors will have to be redefined (capital adequacy requirements, avoidance of banks runs etc.). In all these cases of technological externalities, institutional competition cannot be applied.

In the case of externalities, we have to distinguish clearly between pecuniary and technological externalities. Pecuniary externalities are revealed by the market, for instance falling freight rates with increased economic activity when a railway is set up in a country. With rational expectations, these externalities will be anticipated by the individual agents. Pecuniary externalities can be a matter of concern only if the governmental planning process is superior to coordination via markets. In the basic model of the market for legislation presented earlier, the attraction of mobile factors induces positive effects of an additional income for a country's immobile factors. In this rather broad definition of a pecuniary externality, where third parties are affected only via markets, the marginal conditions are not violated. Therefore, the market for regulation would still yield a Pareto optimal allocation.

Strategic Behaviour and Institutional Competition

Consider a competitive equilibrium of institutional competition, where national governments do not have market power for their regulations. All governments operate so that the marginal costs and marginal benefits of providing legislation are equal. When a national government has reached an optimum, cutting the price for legislation, i.e. lowering taxes, leads to some capital inflow but also to a lower level of public goods supply. In a competitive situation, governments are small so that they cannot influence their marginal costs or benefits by affecting the position of other governments. A move away from the optimum implies a reduction in welfare.

One may argue, however, that the EC's market for legislation is not fully competitive because of the small number of governments. Governments may be viewed as being in the position of oligopolists. They can affect the 'market' price for legislation to some extent, which changes the relations between governments. They can anticipate the pecuniary externalities mentioned earlier. Strategic behaviour may occur, in which a government takes into account the expected reactions of other governments to actions taken by one country. In terms of our reference model, the restrictions on the maximization problem of governments change. Governments may thus behave strategically. By having a low tax on capital, they not only attempt to attract capital, they also anticipate the behaviour of other governments. This may be relevant if an early start, a locking-in of capital, economies of scale or learning effects are relevant. In these cases the action of a government may restrict the decision space of another government. For instance, an early start may limit the possibilities of the other government. Such a strategic, non-cooperative solution will differ from a competitive equilibrium.

If we consider locational competition as a general theory of government behaviour in an international context, a strategic location policy of governments can be included in the theory as a special case. Strategic government behaviour has been analysed extensively in the area of strategic trade policy. Strategic trade policy is interpreted as one way of carrying out strategic locational policy and it can, therefore, be considered as a part of the broader competition of location theory. It is claimed that governments attempt to increase the attractiveness of a location, for instance by paying export subsidies to firms, thereby directly increasing the firms' profits and indirectly enabling them to utilize economies of scale (Brander and Spencer, 1985). In international trade, optimal tariffs, although they are not applicable to the strategic behaviour of national governments inside Europe, are another area of strategic behaviour of countries. The General Agreement on Tariffs and Trade (GATT) represents the major effort to cope with strategic behaviour, such as imposing (optimal) tariffs or subsidizing exports, and to reach a cooperative solution. Without new rules on strategic trade policy in the GATT, countries would predictably try to increase their welfare through strategic behaviour, not taking into account that other countries might implement the same measures or retaliate in other ways. In this case all countries would suffer from strategic behaviour.

Another area of strategic government behaviour relates to externalities that may arise when the international effects of domestic monetary and fiscal stabilization policies are to be evaluated. In a simple Keynesian type of setting the argument is that internal macroeconomic policies generate externalities through trade and capital movements. Since these externalities are not adequately remunerated or sanctioned, the supply of stabilization policies is either too high or too low. Consider a beggar-thy-neighbour policy that stimulates aggregate demand for a country's products through devaluation or import restraints. Or assume that in two countries a low rate of inflation is included in the governments' utility functions. If one country carries out an efficient anti-inflationary policy, this directly changes the production function for low inflation in the other country. The issue is how far these 'externalities' can be internalized by a set of rules, for instance by the simple rule of establishing stability at home, or whether flexible exchange rates insulate a country against the strategic behaviour of other countries, thus delegating the harmonization issue to currency competition. The problems arising in this context, which makes use of a different interpretation of legislation, are discussed in, for instance, Cooper (1985) and Neumann (1990).

An important question is: how relevant is the strategic behaviour of governments towards one another. As was pointed out earlier, in some areas the strategic possibilities of governments are restrained by the opportunity costs they incur through their own strategic behaviour. A government that intends to attract an industry by lowering its environmental standards incurs a degradation of the environment that may not be tolerable to its electorate. Cutting taxes on mobile capital reduces the funds available for financing public goods. Moreover, national governments in Europe are small relative to Europe as a whole; therefore, they cannot get involved in strategic games. Finally, the arguments of an early start, of the locking-in of capital and of economies of scale should not be overemphasized. The existing literature on strategic behaviour of governments is deficient in an important aspect. Strategic behaviour is analysed for only a specific part of government activity, such as capital income taxation, indirect taxation or export subsidization. This limitation is necessary to keep the models manageable. The opportunity costs of government activity are not considered. Consequently, the strategic aspect is grossly overstated. The relevance of strategic behaviour is reduced if additional aspects are taken into consideration, for instance the provision of public goods (Siebert, 1990b).

The macroeconomic strategic behaviour of governments in Europe is limited by a set of rules and other conditions. Assume that an individual country uses its money supply to stimulate aggregate demand. Even in a closed economy, the country will not be able to change its natural rate of unemployment if the level of price rise is anticipated by the trade unions. In the Western European setting, an increase in the money supply may influence expectations of a re-alignment which, in turn, can only be prevented by a rise in the interest rate. A rise in the interest rate will, however, choke off growth. Thus, in the European Monetary System (EMS) purchasing power parity still holds in forming exchange rate expectations, and interest rate parity explains capital flows. Consequently, a country may shoot itself in the foot when it undertakes macroeconomic strategic behaviour. Note that currency competition would clearly limit the manoeuvring space of governments to manipulate the value of their money and this would check governments by the arbitrage of people. Of course, one hopes that the new institutional set-up for a central bank in Europe will not allow strategic behaviour by national governments.

A nuisance for institutional competition is that governments can become 'large' in a strategic sense by product differentiation. An example of product differentiation is the splitting of capital income taxation into taxes on physical capital and taxes on financial capital. A

country like Luxembourg could not attract very much physical capital
even if it did not tax capital at all. It can, however, introduce a very low
tax rate on financial capital and thereby attract large amounts of
financial capital. Congestion does not occur as in the case of physical
capital and the marginal cost of lowering the tax rate may be
negligible. In this case, a country does not even have to be large in a
physical sense to allow for the possibility of strategic behaviour.
Again, this is the general problem of taxation of highly mobile factors.

Strategic Behaviour of Governments and Strategic Behaviour of Firms

If the strategic behaviour of governments is relevant for the concept
of institutional competition, this is because it may destroy the Pareto-
optimality of institutional competition. An interesting problem is the
relationship between strategic behaviour of governments and strategic
behaviour of firms. One important aspect of institutional competition
among governments in Europe is that it reduces the power of national
interest groups, and that it can break a deadlock of inefficient national
regulations resulting from vested interests. In this interpretation,
national governments behave strategically not towards other governments but towards firms. Institutional competition is then interpreted
as reducing the strategic possibilities of firms. This is an efficiency
improving aspect of institutional competition.

In the transition period to Europe 1992 institutional competition
may be a device to reduce the strategic possibilities of firms. But firms
will adjust to the new institutional setting of competing governments
and attempt to behave strategically *vis-à-vis* the governments. This is
especially relevant in a rent-seeking environment in which prices and
incentives are politicized. Moreover, governments may be tempted to
increase the strategic manoeuvring space of their national firms, as in
strategic trade policy. In order to restrain the strategic behaviour of
firms and to ensure competition among firms, a new common set of
rules is necessary in some cases. Competition policy can be
interpreted as such a set of rules.

In an integrated European market, a competitive process between
national anti-trust or competition policies does not work. For many
products, the relevant market is no longer the national but the
European, and the world, market, so that a national anti-trust or
competition policy is not a meaningful concept. Consequently, in the

long run, it cannot be left to national anti-trust or competition policy to check monopolies, mergers, cartels ętc. on a European level. Thus, anti-trust or competition policy must relate to the European market, and it cannot evolve from competition among national competition policies. Only for products with a national distribution can a national competition policy, in the sense of the subsidiary principle, be applied.

According to the interpretation of the European Commission, competition policy overlaps with industrial targeting in the high-tech area. Here a severe risk of *ex ante* harmonization becomes apparent. The sectoral structure will be distorted: large firms in selected industries, benefiting from the single market because of economies of scale and the size of the market, will receive special treatment relative to small and medium-sized firms. Once an industry is chosen for some form of subsidy and permitted to cartelize, the political process is under a self-imposed pressure to make its decision appear to have been right. Moreover, it is not clear how the policy-maker will obtain information on which sector should be treated more favourably. In order to avoid distortions, it would be much better not to use a sector-specific approach, but to improve conditions for research and development in general.

2.7 Environmental Policy – an Example of Institutional Competition?

Environmental policy is an interesting case in the discussion of harmonization versus competition in Western Europe. Should we have a uniform environmental policy in Europe or can environmental policy vary?

Environmental Policy – a Distortion?

An argument very often heard in the public debate is that firms need the same starting conditions in order to compete and that different national environmental regulations would distort competition. This argument states that there is a requirement for the same frame of reference for private decisions, or the same institutional arrangement. In a single market, therefore, firms should have to face the same environmental regulations. This argument of levelling the playing field is, however, a fallacy.

In order to disentangle the political demand that firms need the same conditions everywhere from its economic core, let us differentiate between environmental quality and environmental policy instruments. A decentralized environmental policy can mean two different things (Siebert, 1985):

- differing environmental quality as a target among the individual nations; or
- differing environmental policy instruments expressing environmental scarcity even if identical quality targets prevail.

First of all, Europe does not require the same environmental quality everywhere. This statement clearly depends on the spatial dimensions of environmental systems. If the environment as a public good is of European size, the same environmental quality prevails by definition. However, if environmental media can be interpreted as national public goods, for instance river systems specific to one country or noise pollution, the target can be determined on the national level. Then the country-of-origin principle can be applied. The trade-off between environmental quality as a public consumption good and environmental quality as a receptacle of emissions from production is a purely national problem similar to that of endowment with other factors of production. The national policy process can balance the benefits and costs of preventing pollution, and environmental qualities may differ among countries; environmental policy instruments may differ as well.

Environmental policy instruments, such as emission taxes or pollution licences, represent a cost factor and can be interpreted as a production tax for pollution-intensive activities. The country undertaking environmental policy will negatively affect its comparative and its absolute price advantage. Clearly, the loss of comparative advantage and competitiveness represents an opportunity cost. It can be left to the political preferences of each European country how much it wants to reduce its absolute and comparative price advantage. The principle of the country of origin can be applied (Siebert, 1987, chapter 10). The environment is an immobile factor of endowment, like land and most types of labour. It is quite normal for prices of immobile factors to differ between countries, except for factor prices equalized by trade. This economic reasoning in terms of allocation theory is consistent with the subsidiary principle.

The question arises of whether Europe needs a common minimum ambient quality of the environment. It seems to me that, in principle, it can be left to the European nations to specify the ambient quality that they want to have in their regions. It should be noted that, even assuming identical ambient quality standards, the policy instruments are not necessarily identical. Different explicit or implicit prices for environmental use reflect different scarcities of the environment. For instance, a heavily polluted area requires higher emission taxes. If one decides in favour of a lowest common denominator for environmental quality in Europe, the individual country must still have the option of striving for an environmental quality higher than the common European minimum level. Clearly, the policy instruments used in such a case by individual nations will differ. Differences in licensing represent a strong segmentation of markets whereas differences in prices for emissions (emission taxes, prices for transferable discharge permits) cannot be interpreted as a market segmentation.

Ecological Dumping?

Whereas industry requires a levelling of the playing field, environmentalists fear ecological dumping if environmental policy is delegated to the national political process. The argument goes as follows. If environmental policy is delegated to the individual country, location arbitrage implies that pollution-intensive firms will move to the country with lower environmental restraints, increasing environmental stress there. The same implication will come about even if firms do not move. Countries with a strict environmental policy will increase the costs of production of the pollution-intensive sectors, forcing them to reduce their output. In a country with a less strict environmental policy, the pollution-intensive sectors will improve their comparative advantage; pollution will increase and we have a case of pollute-thy-neighbour-via-trade.

The relocation of firms or the reallocation of factors will not imply a competing down of environmental quality, however, for a number of reasons. The nation negatively affected in environmental quality by its attraction of industry can use environmental policy instruments to protect its environment. Since marginal damages rise progressively with the level of pollution, the country will quickly have an incentive to undertake environmental policy. Moreover, countries attracting new industries can avoid the mistakes that were made in the polluted regions. For instance, a country may not fully utilize the assimilative capacity of its environment, in order to allow for the location and expansion of firms in the future. Thus, it may place an option value on assimilative capacity not being used at a specific moment. Finally, countries would be well advised to consider explicitly the risk of environmental degradation, including irreversibilities, following a preventive principle.

Only if one takes the position that the political process for revealing national preferences is deficient can one claim that the European Community has to take care of national interests. Only if there is a national policy failure can Europe paternalize the national interest. Of course, the presumption would be that a European approach prevents national policy failure.[1] Moreover, the location arbitrage of pollution-intensive firms will imply a harmonization of the level of environmental policy instruments by a competitive political process. Emission taxes will rise in areas attracting pollution-intensive activities or licences will be harder to get. Thus, incentives to avoid emissions will tend to become similar throughout Europe. This also holds if there are strong differences between European nations. Following similar arguments, a country cannot start a competitive race to reduce environmental quality because the opportunity costs of forgone environmental quality limit possible tax cuts (Long and Siebert, 1990).

International Spill-overs

Many environmental problems caused by stationary sources are trans-frontier problems (Rhine pollution, air pollution with sulphur dioxide). In these cases unidirectional or bi-directional interactions between countries exist. In the case of international spill-overs, we have a clear 'technological externality'. The originator of damage shifts costs of abatement to the country receiving the emissions and thus enjoys an artificial comparative advantage. Clearly, trans-frontier

---

[1] Such a presumption seems to be rather arrogant since the democratic legitimation of European policy decisions is – at the moment – rather weak.

pollution represents a distortion. Consequently, institutional competition and the country-of-origin principle cannot be applied. Environmental policy in Europe has to establish an incentive mechanism that takes account of international spill-overs.

In order to solve an international spill-over, we need to specify its allowable level, that is to establish an international diffusion norm. A trans-frontier diffusion norm defines the ambient quality of an environmental system (air, water) when it crosses the border. Diffusion norms have been used in national water quality management, for instance when the water quality of a tributary (such as the Emscher in Germany) has been specified where it enters the main river (the Rhine). Thus, we have practical experience with inter-regional diffusion norms that can easily be extended to the European setting. Problems of the measurement of pollutants ambient in the environment 'at the border' can be solved. This also holds for air pollution, where the ambient quality at the border can be measured by monitoring stations.

The diffusion norm limits the permissible volume of pollutants being exported from a country. Pollutants must therefore be measured at the border of the pollution-exporting country. This procedure prevents political debates on the origin of pollutants that arise if the diffusion norms are defined at the border of the receiving country. For instance, for a country not adjacent to all sources of pollution (such as Denmark), the problem would be to determine where the pollution was coming from. However, monitoring of the pollution transfer at the border of the pollution-exporting country may give rise to moral hazard problems of information, the pollution exporters having an incentive to understate their pollution exports. Once an agreement is reached, the type of policy instruments used to secure the international diffusion norm can be left to the national governments. International diffusion norms are therefore instrumental in decentralizing environmental policy in Europe. This is an important advantage.

Agreement on international diffusion norms requires a cooperative solution with side payments. The diffusion norm is determined by equality of the marginal benefit to the pollutee of reduced pollution and the marginal cost to the polluter of abatement. The pollutee has to make a transfer to the polluter to induce it to abate pollutants. Thus, a type of victim-pays principle is applied and the polluter-pays principle cannot be used. Moreover, the countries truly have to reveal their preferences and provide the correct information. Agreement on international diffusion seems extremely difficult in practice, as the problem of trans-frontier spill-over in the Rhine shows. We have typical free rider behaviour by the upstream polluter (or by the polluter in the upwind location), making a cooperative solution hard to find. Strategic behaviour by the upstream polluter overstating the abatement costs and by the downstream pollutee overstating the damage can usually be observed. We thus have a problem of establishing incentives to reveal information truly.

If the governments of Europe cannot agree on international diffusion norms or introduce an internationally tradeable permit system, the alternative approach is to reduce pollution generally in Europe in order to tackle the diffusion problem. An example is a reduction of pollution by x per cent. This is a rather coarse approach, and it implies a more centralized orientation for environmental policy. Assume, for instance, that one were to raise emission taxes for sulphur dioxide generally in Europe in order to reduce the level of the pollutant ambient in the environment, thereby reducing the transfrontier problem. In this case, abatement clearly would not be cost-minimizing, and the costs of environmental quality would be too high. Definitely, such an approach would not even be second-best.

Special Cases

Emissions from non-stationary sources (transportation) are especially relevant to international interdependence because non-stationary sources can move across borders. Deregulation of the transportation industry and the resulting increased traffic flows aggravate the problem. In the future we may be able to monitor car and truck emissions reliably at reasonable costs. Emission taxes could then be used, and these emission taxes could diverge between nations if the mobile sources did not move across national borders too frequently (tourism). If, however, the sources moved frequently, as in the case of lorries, emission taxes would have to be harmonized. As long as monitoring costs are too high, product norms for transportation equipment are the relevant policy means. These product norms have to be harmonized within Europe in order to prevent market segmentation.

An important issue is the extent to which it can be left to the discretion of an individual country to apply environmental policy instruments specific to its area. In the 'Danish bottle case', the European Court of Justice has upheld the right of an individual country to restrict the import of non-returnable beer cans and bottles for soft drinks and thus has limited the extent of the Cassis-de-Dijon ruling. When the use of products generates externalities (as in the case of the car), nationally differentiated product norms would introduce trade barriers. Therefore, product norms have to be harmonized in Europe. However, we cannot exclude national taxes for pollution-intensive products (or national subsidies for ecological products) if we accept national preferences as a basis in a federalistic structure. Note, however, that national taxes or subsidies only influence the stock of national transportation equipment and cannot affect the movement of vehicles across borders.

Pollutants may be contained in consumer goods (such as the apple); then, too, product norms may be considered, attempting to limit externalities to a third party. The case for or against product norms when pollutants are contained in a product clearly depends on the concept of consumer sovereignty. In quite a few cases, we can rely on consumer sovereignty. If a consumer is well informed and if we can leave it up to the consumer to be informed on product quality over the full range (including toxic material), we do not need product norms. Then, pollutants are basically a private good (or bad) and the Cassis-de-Dijon verdict can be applied. We leave it to the German consumer to drink, or not to drink, beer not produced according to the purity law of 1517. Why worry about non-purities in other goods? Labelling can be used to support consumer sovereignty. In many cases information on the pollution content is sufficient to warn the consumer. Toxic pollutants and pollutants causing severe health damage are a different story. Here product qualities have to be established to protect the consumer, unless one takes the position that it is the consumer's problem to be informed on such pollutants. Product norms[2] represent market segmentation, and they have to be harmonized throughout Europe. Again the issue of a minimum

---

[2] Note that the case of pollutants contained in a product – the case of the apple – is different from the case where pollutants are generated by using a consumption good – the case of the car. In the case of the apple, there are no externalities; in the case of the car, pollutants generated affect a third party.

quality in Europe and national deviation in favour of a higher product quality arises. The importance of product norms can be reduced if liability rules can be established. With liability law, the consumer affected by pollutants in a product can go to court, and court decisions will be anticipated by the originator of a damage. Moreover, an insurance market will develop; thus incentives are introduced to prevent damages. However, transaction costs of liability rules are high; harmonization of liability law in Europe seems to be necessary in order to prevent market segmentation, and this may prove to be extremely difficult.

Hazardous products that enter the market as new products (chemicals, pharmaceutical products) are subject to some form of licensing. This licensing process has to strike a balance between the protection of individual health and environmental quality on the one hand and incentives for innovation on the other hand. With respect to the single market, similar problems arise as in the case of product norms. Applying the Cassis-de-Dijon verdict and allowing different national licensing procedures for some time will reduce market segmentation, but eventualy a *de facto* harmonization will evolve *ex post* by institutional competition.

Market Instruments versus Regulations

In an integrated market, environmental policy has to prevent market segmentation arising from border controls and – more importantly – from market entry barriers due to regulation. Many environmental policy instruments define market entry conditions, such as licensing of facilities, licensing of products and land use planning. It is necessary to realize that price instruments, such as emission taxes, effluent fees and transferable discharge permits, reduce the role of regulatory procedures and thus make market entry easier. From the single market perspective, price instruments therefore have the appeal of reducing market barriers and segmentation. Regulatory approaches such as licensing tend to introduce new barriers, even if they are harmonized in Europe. Moreover, harmonization would be inefficient, for instance if licensing required a European definition of the state of the art in abatement. Prices for environmental use do not introduce such barriers, and it is quite normal for prices for environmental use to differ among European countries because the environment as a receptacle of waste can be viewed as an immobile factor of endowment, and we are accustomed to the idea that prices for immobile factors differ between different regions. This holds even if the targets for ambient levels of environmental quality are identical among European countries.

2.8 Some Implications

In order to ensure the efficiency of institutional competition a set of rules for institutional competition in Europe should be developed. Such an institutional arrangement – *Wettbewerbsordnung* – should be understood not as additional regulations for individual firms but as a system of rules for institutional competition among governments. By accepting these rules, the governments would bind themselves in their future behaviour. The strategic behaviour of governments would be reduced. What would be the major elements of such a system?

1 The right of entry is an important prerequisite of institutional competition. Institutional arrangements should not protect the insider, they should be open. This is a requirement of open markets (Eucken, 1952) and of the open society (Popper, 1944).
2 The right of exit is the mirror image of the right of entry. Both rights allow choice.
3 Freedom of entry and exit implies the free movement of people, goods and factors of production. The arbitrage of consumers, the mobility of labour and the mobility of capital are important ingredients of institutional competition.
4 With free entry being an important prerequisite of institutional competition, the EC should improve its openness to the rest of the world so that successful legislation can attract mobile resources from there. Institutional competition inside the EC requires free trade with the outside.
5 In addition, remaining market segmentations should be abolished because they distort the allocation of resources and open up possibilities for strategic behaviour. For instance, governments should not be allowed to use public procurement for strategic purposes.

6 We cannot rely on institutional competition when externalities are involved, such as trans-frontier pollution, and when a common frame of reference for Europe is needed, as in the case of competition policy. New rules, including new property rights, have to be established.
7 In the case of international externalities, rules of internalization have to be agreed upon. These rules attempt to extend the fiscal equivalence concept to nations. In the case of the environment, ambient diffusion norms or the polluter-pays principle are cases in point.
8 A European competition policy for firms is needed in order to avoid strategic behaviour of firms. Institutional competition of EC governments must be protected from EC-wide monopolies or cartels because a non-competitive demand side would impair the efficiency of the market for legislation.

In principle, institutional competition is an efficient means of integration. It is a useful device for revealing the benefits and costs of alternative institutional arrangements and for freeing regulations from vested interests. It is a strategy to evaluate the opportunity costs of government activities and thus to increase government efficiency.

Since institutional competition assesses overall government performance, the possibilities for governments to behave strategically in one area at the expense of other areas are effectively reduced. There will be many chances for arbitrage by households and firms in the case of institutional competition as long as those who benefit from government activities and those who pay for it are not identical. For governments it is therefore important to look for institutional arrangements that establish this identity. The process of institutional competition is a driving force to make users and payers identical. Within nations, internalization of benefits and costs can be obtained by benefit taxation, user charges, other forms of private financing and privatization.

The country-of-origin principle in the Cassis-de-Dijon ruling of the European Court of Justice may prove to be an important institutional device for harmonization in Europe. With mutual recognition of the institutional arrangements of the country of origin, harmonization can be delegated to a competitive process between institutional arrangements. This process will be open-ended, and harmonization will occur only *ex post*. An important ingredient of this process is the arbitrage of households and firms taking advantage of institutional differences and thus establishing political pressure for harmonization *ex post*.

The harmonization issue should not be confounded with equalizing endowment. Countries are differently endowed with factors of production such as labour, land and nature. We cannot harmonize the sunshine in Europe. Differences in endowment tend to require different prices for immobile factors (unless we are in the Heckscher–Ohlin world of perfect factor price equalization). Institutional competition is about attracting mobile factors of production, such as capital, to the immobile endowment factor.

3

The Transformation of Eastern Europe

3.1 The Collapse of Central Planning – a Result of Institutional Competition

The year 1985 was a time of change for Europe, both in the West and in the East. In Western Europe, the Delors initiative for Europe 1992, which started in 1985 with the White Paper of 300 single steps, has given new momentum to the EC. The liberalization of capital flows and services, the replacement of the unanimity rule in the Council of Ministers by majority voting in a weighted form for the larger part of the 300 directives, and the Cassis-de-Dijon ruling handed down by the European Court of Justice will reduce market segmentation and will lead to a more intense economic and political integration. Institutional competition and the Delors initiative have stimulated the imagination in Europe and have already contributed to an increase in investment activity, including the reorganization of firms and the relocation of some of their plants. In the modern world, with a rapid international diffusion of information, a mutual penetration of countries by means of mass communication and decreasing costs of relocation, this positive development in Western Europe was observed by people in Eastern Europe and was very attractive to the Eastern European countries. The developments in Eastern Europe might not have taken place if Latin America had been its neighbour. Thus, the democratic revolutions of the year 1989 might well be regarded as a result of institutional competition between Eastern and Western European countries.

While Western Europe gained new economic momentum, Eastern Europe experienced an Orwellian crisis of central planning and socialism. The planning system had proved to be completely inefficient and unable to provide enough goods for people. Except for the privileged *nomenklatura* (people selected by the Communist Party for key posts), the target of equality seemed to have been realized – albeit at a very low level. As Churchill once remarked, 'The inherent vice of capitalism is the unequal sharing of blessings, the inherent virtue of socialism is the equal sharing of miseries'.

The punch line is that governments in open societies have to consider the risk of arbitrage and of factor emigration. Before the opening of the 'iron curtain', however, potentially mobile factors in Eastern Europe were unable to react by location arbitrage. As a result, pressure in the East accumulated over the years, finally leading to the revolutions we all witnessed. The political demand for individual freedom and open societies, for the social market economy and democracy, for a new orientation of economic, social and political life, is sweeping away old and rigid structures and changing the institutional setting of Eastern Europe. Starting in Poland and Hungary, the new political demand extended to the Baltic States, the GDR and Czechoslovakia. Communist parties in these countries lost their political power. Last but not least, the necessity of institutional reform became apparent in the USSR. The common feature of the developments in all Eastern European countries is the failure of the central planning approach and the need for decentralization. The need for a new economic institutional arrangement goes hand in hand with the political demand for individual rights and democratic forms of government. We are witnesses to a major historical change.

The year 1985 – the year of the White Paper in Western Europe – was also the year of Gorbachev. He must have recognized that the status of the USSR as a developing country – an Upper Volta with atomic weapons, as Helmut Schmidt once remarked – had to be changed. Even though the direction of change in the USSR is still completely undetermined, 1985 was an important caesura in both the West and the East and will be an important year in the history books.

3.2 The Disparity with the West: Starting Conditions in the East

Statistical information on economic conditions in Eastern Europe is incomplete and distorted. According to international statistics available before the revolutions of 1989, some of the Eastern European countries fared pretty well (see table A5 in the appendix). For instance, CIA data (1989) estimated income per head in the GDR at US\$ 12,634, which amounted to the average of the EC countries in 1988, and was not too different from Western Germany's (US\$ 14,192). UN sources (1989) showed a similarly high income per head in the GDR, and the widely quoted Summers and Heston (1988) data put Eastern Germany on a par with Sweden.

Table 3.1   GNP per capita in selected Eastern European countries, 1988

	Population (million)	GNP per capita (US\$)
Hungary	10.6	2 460
Poland	37.9	1 860
Yugoslavia	23.6	2 320
OECD average		17 400

Source: World Bank, 1990b, p. 179

We have become aware that these data were false. World Bank (1990) data (see table 3.1), probably the most reliable in the field, but only available for Hungary, Poland and Yugoslavia, indicate that income per capita in Hungary (US\$ 2460) and Yugoslavia (US\$ 2320) in 1988 reached only half that in Greece (US\$ 4800). Poland's income per capita (US\$ 1860) was only half that of Portugal (US\$ 3650). It is not true that living conditions in the rich socialist countries, the GDR and Czechoslovakia, were on a par with those in less advanced nations in Western Europe. Moreover, environmental damage was ignored, medical facilities were inappropriate, housing was poor and social security was insufficient.

Economic conditions in the region of the former GDR and Eastern Europe vary between the countries, but some features are common:

- inefficiency of production and a partially obsolete capital stock;
- a distorted trade structure oriented towards Comecon and not the international market;

- product qualities not satisfying international demand, so that firms are not competitive;
- a 'marked deterioration in the efficiency of capital investment and slower growth in productivity' in the 1980s (Institute of International Finance, 1990). The incremental capital output ratio (ICOR) rose, indicating that more investment was necessary to produce an additional unit of output;
- a fall in productivity growth rates from 5 per cent in the 1970s to 2 per cent in the 1980s (Institute of International Finance, 1990);
- a poor environmental record – for instance, Czechoslovakia and the ex-GDR have the highest per capita sulphur dioxide emissions in the world.

The growth rate of gross domestic product per capita in the Eastern European countries declined considerably in the period 1950–88 (figure 3.1), especially from 1970 to 1988. There is also a long-run decline in the growth rates of gross domestic product per capita in Western countries, but the decline in Eastern Europe is more pronounced. Moreover, the gap in relative development level (with the US real gross domestic product per capita being used as the base) has increased more than slightly. For this analysis, data from the CIA, PlanEcon, and Summers and Heston (1988) have been used.

Even the policy domain, where centrally planned economies are expected by some to out-perform market economies, especially in income distribution, did not yield the intended results. 'Post-tax income distribution in the Soviet Union, for example' – in contrast to Churchill's dictum – 'does not appear to be more egalitarian than in many Western European countries' (International Monetary Fund, 1990, p. 68). The *Economist* (28 April, 1990, p. 6) has illustrated the situation:

> McDonalds, an American fast-food company, opened its first Russian establishment, in Moscow's Pushkin Square. A hamburger plus accessories costs six roubles, which is roughly $10 at the official exchange rate; more to the point, it is half a day's wages for most workers. A queue trails back and forth across the square; a wait of four hours is typical. An afternoon queueing in the cold to spend a morning's pay on a hamburger. That is as good a measure of economic failure as any.

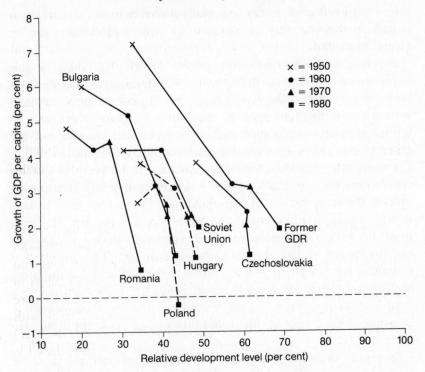

Figure 3.1   Economic growth and development levels in
Eastern Europe.

Relative development level is shown on a scale with US real GDP per capita = 100. Note that
the relative position to the US is overestimated.
Source: Heitger, 1990.

3.3 Three Major Areas of Reform

Many books have been written on the issue of how to transform a
capitalist economy into a communist one and even more books have
been written on why one should do so. But we have no recipe for the
transition from a socialist economy into a market economy. The basic
question is: how do you transform a socialist centrally planned
economy into a market economy in which individual preferences
count and in which firms react to prices? Obviously, central planning
has to be given up, and the economic system has to be completely
revised. The basic mechanism of allocation must be the market and

prices must reflect scarcities, especially scarcities in world markets. It is only in this way that the opportunity cost of production can be clearly evaluated.

Steering the economy with prices already has quite a few implications. It implies that government trading monopolies, on both the import and the export sides, have to go. At the same time, with national markets open to the world economy there will be arbitrage in the commodity markets between one country and the other if the prices of tradeable commodities differ by too much. Consequently, subsidies for tradeables have to be given up. Prices also require decentralization and the autonomy of organizational sub-units of the economy, i.e. of households and firms. They must be free to react to supply and demand and to the forces of the market. Firms must be fully responsible for their economic decisions, so they can no longer be bailed out by the government. This means that economic losses have to be internalized to the firm and that the 'soft-budget constraint' for firms (Kornai, 1980) has to be turned into a hard-budget constraint. Firms must be liable for their economic decisions. One aspect of this is that they can go bankrupt if they are not viable.

Not only commodity markets but also factor markets must be steered by prices. This holds for land, labour, natural resources and capital. The capital market is especially crucial for a market economy. The capital market determines whether it is worthwhile to put financial funds into a firm. If a firm is viable, it can attract capital and expand. If it does not succeed in attracting additional funds, and if profits are negative, it will eventually have to disappear from the market. The capital market provides evaluation of firms and in this way controls management. It is an important steering mechanism in a capitalist economy.

There are three major areas of reform that are interlinked but that can nevertheless be distinguished: the institutional infrastructure, monetary stabilization and real adjustment on the micro-level, that is in firms.

The institutional infrastructure relates to the rules to be followed, to what the Freiburg school calls the *Wirtschaftsordnung*, to the legal system, to contract law, to company law including the rules holding for joint-stock companies and other companies, to the two-tier banking system, to the independence of the central bank, to property rights and to the demarcation of government and the private sector. In short, this is the economic constitution and the laws around it that specify the rules of the economic system.

One of the most important elements of the institutional infrastructure is property rights. Property rights define the rules for using scarce goods and resources. They are the crucial institutional device by which decisions can be decentralized. The economic unit that enjoys the benefits of a decision should also bear the opportunity costs. Property rights are a device to satisfy this condition. They privatize the benefits and the costs of economic decisions. It should be noted that the equality of marginal benefit and marginal costs only holds for the marginal transaction in a market. In a market with many buyers and many sellers there will always be buyers with a willingness to pay higher than the market price, who thus receive a consumer's surplus. Similarly, there are suppliers on the supply side who are prepared to sell at a lower price, and who thus receive a producer's surplus. Producer's and consumer's surplus indicate the advantage of a transaction to the parties concerned.

It need not be stressed that private property is an important motivational force for exploitation of the best use of a resource, and, together with the market mechanism, it is a driving force in the search for new information, including new technology. Property rights and competition are thus an exploratory device in Hayek's (1968) sense. Property rights are also an incentive to the taking of a long-run view of resource use. Transferability of a property right gives a capital value to the property, and the capital value can be cashed in by the next generation. Thus, property rights represent an intertemporal link between generations, even without bequest. Of course, this intertemporal role of property rights clearly depends on the certainty of the property rights.

Macroeconomic or monetary reform is the second area of reform in the Eastern European countries. A stable and convertible currency is a mandatory precondition for the functioning of the price mechanism and for efficient allocation. If price level stability is violated, it is difficult to introduce or stick to the convertibility of the home currency, which is a prerequisite for capital flows and the exploitation of comparative advantages. Moreover, there is a risk that eventually runaway inflation must be controlled by a price stop; then the market mechanism does not function properly any more, and the whole reform attempt may have been in vain. Political obstacles to new reforms will have increased.

From the institutional side, monetary stability requires the establishment of a two-tier banking system, with private banks and an autonomous central bank. Moroever, it implies that government expenditures can no longer be financed by printing money. With respect to governments, a new tax system has to be developed and a new social security system, including unemployment insurance, has to be designed. Monetary stabilization is not only linked to the financing of the government, it is also influenced by wage policy, because changes in wages define the manoeuvring space of the monetary authorities. Thus, the arrangement of the labour market and a definition of the role of trade unions are intertwined with monetary stabilization.

Countries starting with a monetary overhang (too much money chasing too few goods) – such as Poland, with a hyperinflation rate of 650 per cent in 1989, and the USSR, with a current monetary overhang and *de facto* price rise – face the problem that structural and institutional reform must be combined with a reduction of nominal absorption in order to get a stable price level. Reducing absorption means squeezing consumption and government spending. Tradeables must become more expensive so that production of tradeables increases and demand is reduced (expenditure switching) and so that an excess supply of tradeables for exports is generated.

The third area of reforms is at the micro-level. Markets imply competition, which means that government monopolies have to go and new organizational structures have to be found for firms that were monopolies. As a rule, each industry was organized as a single firm with a clearly segmented market. For instance, shipbuilding was organized as one firm. A publisher of children's books was not allowed to publish an economics text. Each industry had a neatly protected market for itself, which was assured by the demarcation of the industry's market from other sectors. Moreover, the Eastern European philosophy of international specialization from above implied that national industries were also protected from international competitors.

3.4 The Restructuring and Privatization of Firms

The restructuring of existing firms consists of three aspects that are interlinked. First, how can new smaller organizational units be defined? Second, how can existing firms be made efficient and economically viable? Third, in what way can firms be privatized?

The dismantling of the state-owned enterprises implies the splitting up of firms into smaller units. Organizational sub-units of state monopolies should have the option to declare themselves legally independent units. Moreover, an explicit government policy should force existing monopolies to dismantle themselves into smaller organizational units or should dissolve them by law. This approach was followed in the German case, where 321 *Kombinats* were turned into 8000 legally independent firms comprising 40,000 plants. Breaking up government monopolies into smaller legally independent units does not solve the problem of making these new units efficient, but a smaller unit is easier to handle and more flexible.

Making existing firms efficient requires a spectrum of measures ranging over a wide area. First, a firm has to establish the product or product set that it can sell in the market. The firm might have to establish a new product. Second, firms have tended to be as self-sufficient as possible, producing their own inputs in order not to depend on delivery from other suppliers. The production of these intermediate inputs may have to be given up. This may also apply to the repair department, the transportation division and other functions. Third, new production technology will be necessary in most cases, which requires investment. Fourth, marketing has to be undertaken and a distribution and service system has to be built up. There are many other aspects of firms' adjustment, including organizational changes, the introduction of new management techniques and, in most cases, reduction of the workforce.

The issue of the shape of new organizational units is intermingled with the issue of the ownership of firms and control of managers. Firms should be privatized. The organizational structure of industry and the ownership of firms are the core problems for structural adjustment and for a dynamic change of the socialist economies in a Schumpeterian sense. The big issue is which institutional arrangement can achieve privatization. In Poland and Hungary, 90 per cent of industry is in state hands. In Czechoslovakia, expropriated small firms will be given back to their previous owners. Since late 1990, smaller businesses in crafts, services and retail trade have been auctioned in the so-called 'small privatization'. The privatization of larger firms is scheduled for 1991.

Privatization has to provide a mechanism by which private owners are established. It must make sure that:

• decisions in firms are dominated by economic considerations;
• a dynamic process of structural change is possible;
• capital will be allocated to its best use in the economy; and
• managers are controlled by the capital market.

Additionally, privatization can be used to establish a new middle class of property owners and to raise people's interest in their stake in firms. Of course, solutions to the privatization issue will differ depending on the weights put on the different targets. Moreover, solutions may vary with respect to the time-scale required.

The most comprehensive goal of privatization is to privatize firms and to establish a new ownership class. In this case, the old firms must be given or sold to the population. Privatization could be used to reduce the monetary overhang. In any case, ownership titles must be transferable so that a capital market can be established. Moreover, foreigners must be allowed to buy these transferable titles so that new (foreign) capital can be attracted and eventually invested in the economy. In the initial allocation or sale of property titles, some of the ownership titles may have to be open to foreign investors.

To give company shares exclusively to the workers of a firm has the disadvantages that:

• the risk of unemployment and the risk of capital loss are centred on one group, implying rent-seeking by that group in the political arena;
• workers will dominate the economic decisions of the firm and will impede structural change;
• workers tend to be interested in quick pay-outs and do not have an interest in providing capital;
• the total wealth is not equally distributed to the whole population.

The Yugoslav experience supports these concerns, especially the deficient capital accumulation. If company shares are given to the workers, the shares should be transferable, so that a capital market can quickly be established. This is equivalent to giving an option to workers to acquire shares and making the option transferable. In order to attract foreign capital, it is recommended that a portion of shares can be purchased by foreigners.

Governments are tempted to mix privatization with structural policy. Such an approach will fail because structural policy will attempt to smooth the transition for individual firms, protecting employment by subsidizing old lines of production and by intervening in the market mechanism that has to be created. People should be protected by social policy and not by structural policy. Clearly, privatization should not be mixed with structural policy. Care must be taken that institutional arrangements for privatization do not perpetuate government ownership (e.g. giving property titles to communities), that big financial trusts with political interests (and rent-seeking) are not established and that the managers are not controlled by workers' councils, but by the capital market.

In terms of organizational problems, a privatization agency, such as the German Treuhand, can be created and charged with privatizing the firms (and in the case of Treuhand the additional highly questionable role of making firms efficient). In a way this approach has the potential advantage of separating the policy arena from privatization; however, there will be strong political pressure on Treuhand. The organization charged with privatization should be independent.

A possible procedure would be to establish several holding companies for the whole country's government property in order to have competition among the privatization agencies (Kostrzewa et al., 1989; Siebert and Schmieding, 1990). The allocation of existing firms to the privatization agencies must be done on a random basis. The privatization agencies should be dissolved within a specific time. Moreover, incentives must be introduced that ensure that the privatization agency will eventually disappear. The holding company would have the right to define new units, but existing parts of firms with some organizational autonomy would have the right to initiate the process of privatization, for instance by finding a buyer or using a management buy-out for a specific organizational sub-system. In order to prevent a sell-out, the sale should be announced publicly; if within a time span of two months no other bidder showed up, the privatization deal would go through. Possibly, outside investors could be granted the right to initiate a bid, which then would be tested in an auction.

A voucher system may be a way to reduce the power of the privatization agency. The voucher is an ownership title to all government-owned firms. In this approach a voucher is given to each citizen. The voucher must be transferable. Once new firms have been formed, their shares are exchanged for vouchers. In this case, privatization is obtained by distributing vouchers, and there is pressure on the privatization process from below, because voucher owners eventually want to have shares. The role of the privatization agency can be reduced by the establishment of markets in which the price of shares in units of vouchers is determined. The voucher system attempts to distribute assets equally among the population. Its disadvantage is that it will take time for explicit ownership of specific firms to be established and new management to be introduced. Moreover, it does not inject new capital quickly. An alternative approach is to privatize firms by selling shares right away, letting the receipts go to the firms. Then the firm receives an injection of capital and new owners; eventually, new management will be introduced by the new established owners. This procedure cannot be followed if the sale of shares is intended to reduce the monetary overhang and if new management has to be introduced quickly in order to turn around the firm.

The conditions for privatization vary between countries. In the German case it is important to privatize quickly and to use privatization as a vehicle to attract private capital quickly. Unlike other Eastern European countries, Eastern Germany has the same currency and the same institutional setting as Western Germany, and therefore it has a great potential for massive capital flows, which must be tapped.

Methods used to privatize firms can be ordered on a continuum. Access of firms to the stock market establishes a reliable evaluation of the capital value of a firm by many buyers, including a market judgement of economic viability. In the German case, this would, in principle, represent a possibility for some viable East German firms, but access to the stock market requires many preconditions that are not fulfilled. Moreover, this is a time-consuming process. At the other extreme of the continuum, there is 'informal selling' as a way to privatize, with one party or only few on the buyer's side. Here the advantage is that informal selling does not require much time, but the buyer's side of the market is too 'thin', giving rise to the possibility of too low a selling price. These two ways of privatizing firms – the stock market and informal selling – are two extremes of a continuum. In between is a formal bidding process, like the one used in mergers and acquisitions in the USA. This seems to be the appropriate approach for Treuhand.

In the German case, the establishment of a semi-stock market for East German firms with a less formal stock exchange admission regulation (Börsenzulassungs-Verordnung) may be a possibility. This would mean that firms had easier access to the capital market, and could privatize themselves without the help of Treuhand. Apparently, this way is only possible when firms are somewhat viable. An issue may be that this procedure makes it easier for the old management to stay in power.

An important aspect of the restructuring of industry is the creation of new firms. As a matter of fact, it is more important to have new firms than to restructure the old. New firms will soak in workers from the inefficient old firms and will solve the adjustment problem automatically. For instance, in Western Germany, 3.7 million employees were released from the agricultural sector during 1950–90 and were taken in by the manufacturing and strongly expanding service sectors. Thus, conditions must be established so that new firms can come into existence. Market entry barriers should be abolished, location space must be supplied and finance must be available, especially for new and small firms. Thus, the semi-stock market or a type of venture capital market should be open to the new firms. It is worth recalling that the majority of employment occurs in the small firm: 78 per cent of employment in manufacturing industries in Germany is in firms with less than 500 employees (Schmidt, 1990).

3.5 The J-curve of Output and the u-curve of Employment

In the adjustment of output and employment the inefficiencies of the old planning system will be clearly revealed. From the German and the Polish experience we know that the transition from a planning to a

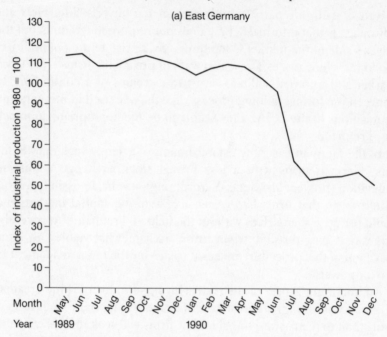

(a) East Germany

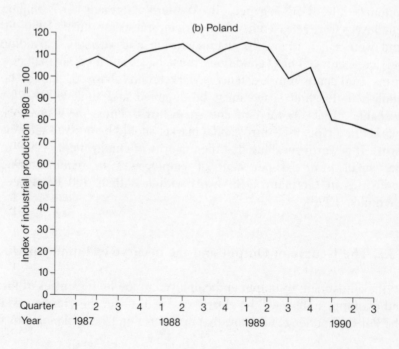

(b) Poland

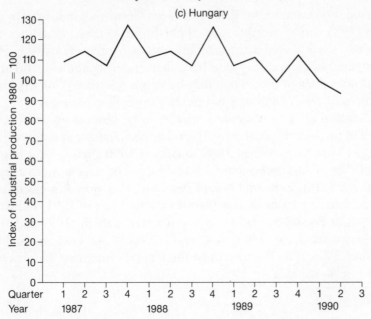

Figure 3.2   The J-curves of industrial output 1989–90 in (a)
Eastern Germany, (b) Poland and (c) Hungary.

Sources: (a) Gemeinsames Statistisches Amt der Neuen Bundesländer, 1990, Statistisches Bundesamt, 1991; (b) The *Economist* Intelligence Unit, Poland Country Report no. 4, 1990; (c) The *Economist* Intelligence Unit, Hungary Country Report no. 4, 1990

market economy is associated with an initial decline in output and employment – with a J-curve, in which output first falls into a dip, a valley or a deep gorge, and then starts to rise when the incentive mechanism of the market economy begins to play, eventually reaching higher levels than before the fall. The exact shape of this curve is not known, but it is relevant for the political economy of transition. Clearly, the shape of the J-curve depends on the inefficiency of the existing firms, on the speed and methods of privatization, on the speed with which new firms will come into existence and on the conditions of the process of restructuring. Moreover, macroeconomic variables, such as the exchange rate and the wage rate, are relevant.

Statistical measurement of the J-curve is loaded with difficulties. The transition implies a sizeable change in the price system, and indices of production use the obsolete price weights of the pre-reform period. For instance, for data on Eastern Germany's industrial output the 1985 price weights are applied. Of course, quantities are themselves distorted because of false prices. Moreover, statistics from the planning period may have been deliberately beautified, and gross and net values of production may be falsely specified. Consequently, indices of production may not be meaningfully compared.

Neglecting these objections, we can so far observe only the falling part of the J-curve. In the East German case, industrial output fell by 50 per cent from August 1989 to August 1990 (figure 3.2a) despite subsidies of an unprecedented magnitude. The data seem to suggest that the fall in industrial output has come to a stop, but closures of large firms were due to take place in the first half of 1991. Industrial output in Poland has fallen, as the quarterly data for 1989 and 1990 show (figure 3.2b). There is a smaller decline for Hungary in 1990 (figure 3.2c). The falling part of the J-curve cannot yet be observed for Czechoslovakia for 1990.

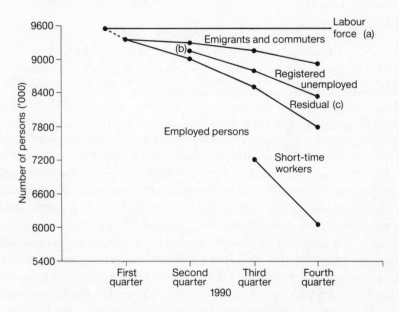

Figure 3.3   The u-curve of employment in Eastern Germany, 1989–90.

[a] Fourth quarter 1989. [b] June 1990. [c] Residual includes, for example, people in early retirement and unregistered job-seekers.

The J-curve of output will be accompanied by a u-curve of employment (a u-curve because employment cannot exceed 100 per cent). The exact shape of the u-curve depends crucially on the adjustment of real wages. Whereas workers in Poland are apparently willing to accept temporary real wage cuts, real wages in Eastern Germany are strongly influenced by the West German labour market. Hence, the falling part of the Polish u-curve will probably be flatter than that of the East German u-curve. In East Germany firms will adjust employment more dramatically because labour productivity has to match the high real wages. Unemployment in Eastern Germany rose from 140,000 in June 1990 to 642,200 in December and 840,000 in April 1991. The number of people on short-time work amounted to 656,000 in June 1990 and 2 million in April 1991 (figure 3.3). Moreover, net emigration rose from 12,000 per month in May and June 1990 to 28,000–31,000 in July, August and September and is estimated 15,000 per month in the first quarter of 1991. Note that the initial level of employment given in figure 3.3 for April 1989 is distorted and cannot be considered to be the full employment level of East Germany in a market economy.

3.6 Sequencing

The sequencing of the steps of reforms is a major issue. There is fierce debate about whether the transition should be done in a gradual process or in a big leap forward, where the crucial reforms take place as a shock to the system, either simultaneously or at relatively short times after each other.

As a rough rule, the institutional infrastructure (contract and company law, property rights, two-tier banking system etc.) has to be established first. As a second step, the basic micro-reforms must follow. The micro-reforms may be split up into two different aspects, their start and their implementation. The start of the micro-reforms includes decentralization of the economy, autonomous decision-making by firms, which in this stage are not yet in private hands, introduction of markets instead of central planning and free market entry for new firms. This stage must be connected with or closely followed by the freeing of prices in the most important goods markets. At the same time, the country must be opened to the world economy and subsidies for tradeables must be abolished. The other aspects of implementing the micro-reforms, such as introducing the capital market, de-monopolizing firms (e.g. dismantling the *Kombinats*), privatizing firms and having new firms enter the market, will require more time (figure 3.4).

Monetary stabilization must not be too distant from the micro-reforms. However, the means of monetary stabilization influences the optimal time positions of the micro-reforms and monetary stabilization. There are two different approaches. One approach is to reduce the monetary overhang before (or simultaneously with) the micro-reforms. Then monetary stabilization precedes the micro-reforms or occurs simultaneously. The other approach is to consider inflation as a temporary option for reducing the monetary overhang before stabilization bites. In this case, prices are freed while the monetary overhang still exists. But inflation involves the risk of giving a reason for wage increases, of distorting the allocation mechanism, eventually requiring a price stop and consequently leading to a failure of the transition process itself. If that is a real danger, monetary stabilization must not be separated too much from the micro-reforms. As already stated, monetary stabilization is linked to the independence of the central bank and to the rules of government finance, including the design of the tax system. Finally, real adjustment at the micro-level of firms, such as de-monopolization, privatization and the creation of new firms, will take considerable time.

In Figure 3.4 an attempt is made to show the analytical structure of the basic reforms in the transition process. Except for the restructuring of firms, which must be thought of in terms of years (and depending on the country involves one or two decades), all the reforms must be close to each other in time, and here we should think in terms of months and not years. The relative positions of specific measures in time depend on the options chosen, as was explained with respect to monetary stabilization. Some measures, such as the specifics of contract laws, can take time too, but the basic rules of contract law must be established at the beginning. In the German economic and monetary reform of 1948 a 'guideline law' – *Leitsätzegesetz* – was used to define the main principles to be specified later, such as the right to open up a business (*gewerbefreiheit*), open and competitive markets, anti-trust principles, bankruptcy rules etc.

This picture of transition can be made more specific by studying the sequencing possibilities in some detail. There is a question of

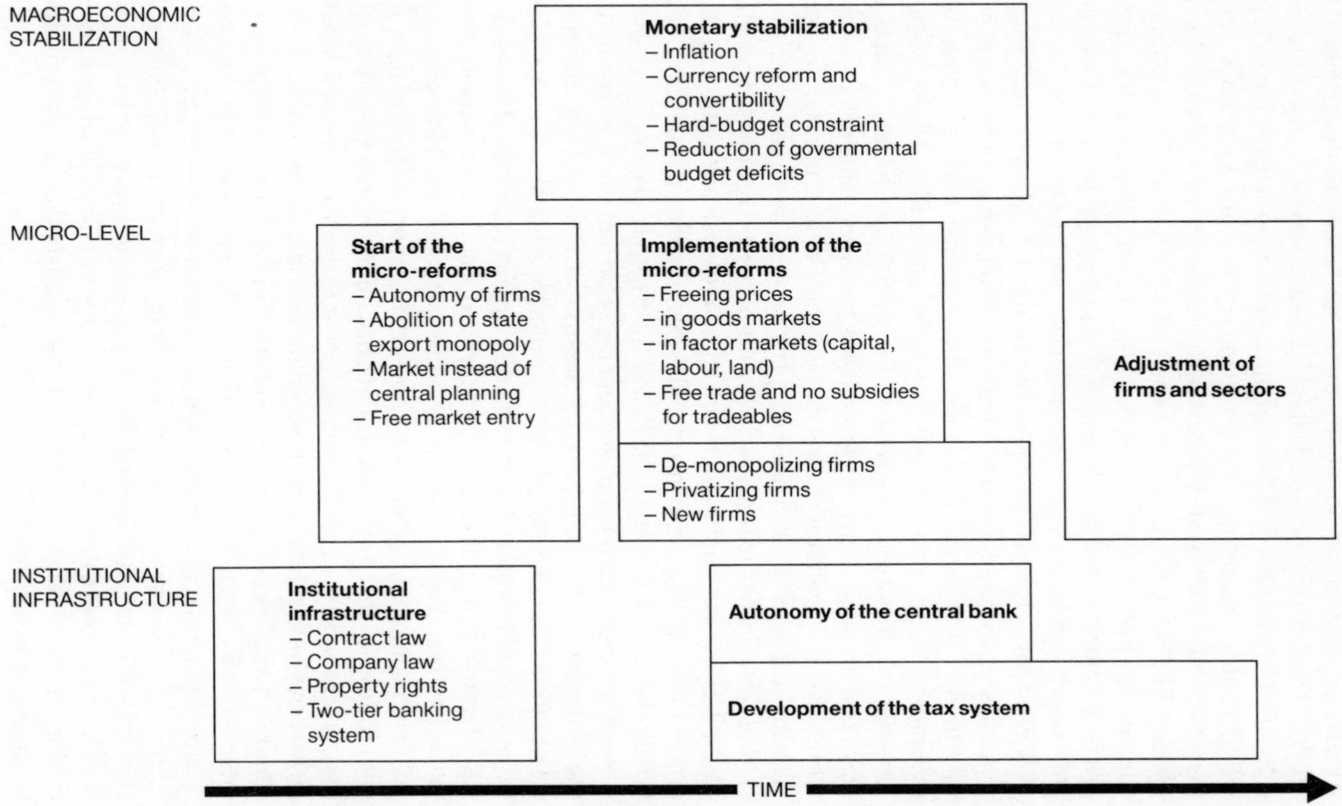

MACROECONOMIC
STABILIZATION

Monetary stabilization
– Inflation
– Currency reform and
  convertibility
– Hard-budget constraint
– Reduction of governmental
  budget deficits

**Adjustment of
firms and sectors**

MICRO-LEVEL

**Start of the
micro-reforms**
– Autonomy of firms
– Abolition of state
  export monopoly
– Market instead of
  central planning
– Free market entry

**Implementation of the
micro-reforms**
– Freeing prices
– in goods markets
– in factor markets (capital,
  labour, land)
– Free trade and no subsidies
  for tradeables

– De-monopolizing firms
– Privatizing firms
– New firms

INSTITUTIONAL
INFRASTRUCTURE

**Institutional
infrastructure**
– Contract law
– Company law
– Property rights
– Two-tier banking
  system

Autonomy of the central bank

Development of the tax system

TIME

Figure 3.4 The sequencing of transition in Eastern European economies.

whether a sequencing possibility exists for some sectors (Edwards, 1989). Thus, some non-tradeables (housing, some transportation) can still be subsidized. However, the option used by China (Lal, 1990) of introducing the market economy first for agriculture and then for crafts and small industry may no longer be sufficient for a country like the USSR, because such an option would be too time-consuming. People are no longer willing to wait. Nevertheless, free prices for agricultural goods and individual property in agricultural land might still be an improvement in the Soviet Union.

A regional sequencing is possible in the USSR, with individual republics such as the Baltic states undertaking a more intensive reform in a big jump. Politically, this regional approach may be considered as an aspect of the inevitable unravelling of the Soviet Empire, and historical analogies to the British and French Empires may come to mind. Such an approach is very promising in economic terms, and it is politically attractive for the Baltic states. Of course, allowing regional preferences to play implies less power for the central state, just as federalism in Western Europe restrains Brussels. In the USSR, this conflict between some regional autonomy and the power of the central state involves the risk of political instability – de Gaulle once said that the USSR had 12 Algerias ahead.

Another specific aspect of sequencing relates to the opening up of the economy to the international division of labour. One question relates to the extent to which the transition to a market economy may be coupled with import duties and other import restraints. Theoretically, many arguments can be put forward for first introducing the market to the closed economy and then opening up. However, the political economy of protection shows that import restraints tend to stay. Industries that are inefficient because of the planning system will have a chance to organize themselves into pressure groups when tariffs and other forms of protection are introduced. The Latin American experience of import substitution and the protection of infant export sectors suggests that it is not advisable to use 'temporary' protection in the transition to an open economy. With respect to the convertibility of the home currency, full 'internal convertibility' is instrumental in giving credibility to a monetary stabilization programme. A strict monetary stabilization programme, aiming at price level stability and the hard-budget constraint for firms, requires convertibility.

A technical argument in the parcelling of reforms is the economist's playground of the second-best. According to this concept, an optimum may not be realized, if one of the n conditions for its existence is fulfilled, when at the same time some of the other conditions are not satisfied. The theory of the second-best proposes that satisfying an additional condition while others are still violated may lead away from an optimum. Unfortunately, the theory of the second-best has been applied to the Western type of static allocation problems, but not to the transition from a socialist system to a market economy. Most specifically, second-best arguments do not take into account the political economy of transition, such as the vested interest of the *nomenklatura* or the endogenous political dynamics of the transformation process.

Four arguments can be put forward in favour of a big leap, such as the Polish approach:

1 Some of the reforms are deeply interlinked and must be carried out more or less simultaneously.
2 For investment to be made, the reforms must be credible. This means that they must be irreversible. Gradual reforms do not prevent the expectation that the planning system and the *nomenklatura* will come back. Consequently, reforms must be done in a discrete way.
3 The population, having been exposed to too many empty promises in the past, is no longer willing to wait.
4 The reforms must catch the attention of people, change their expectations and behaviour. This cannot easily be done in a gradual approach.

Finally it is worth remembering that 'you cannot cross a chasm in two jumps'.

3.7 The Countries

Eastern European countries do not have conditions as favourable as those in Eastern Germany:

1 They have to develop their own institutional infrastructures, whereas Eastern Germany has adopted the Federal Republic's constitution and basic economic laws.

2 They have to solve the problem of foreign debt (Poland US$ 42.7 billion, Hungary US$ 20.2 billion, USSR US$ 54 billion; World Bank, 1990; IMF, 1990), whereas East Germany's foreign debt has been taken over by the united Germany.
3 They have to create their own hard and convertible currencies through painful stabilization programmes.
4 They will not have the advantage of sizeable transfers, either private investment or governmental transfers. Even taking into account that Eastern European countries can use the exchange rate as a shock absorber and can insulate their wages from abroad, institutional change and structural adjustment will be much more difficult than in the ex-GDR.

The state of reform differs between the countries. Poland has so far followed a big leap strategy, including a strict stabilization programme to fight an inflation rate that reached 650 per cent in 1989. The inflation rate was down to 4–5 per cent per month in late 1990, mounting to 12 per cent in January 1991. The zloty was stable relative to the dollar, and shelves were full. But industrial output in 1990 was roughly 21 per cent below that of a year before. Unemployment has increased. Privatization of firms and the restructuring of industry have been dragging because of the strong influence of the workers' councils. Nevertheless, privatization may be speeded up considerably by the government of Prime Minister Bielecki. Future prospects will depend crucially on the extent to which the Polish government sticks to the transition strategy.

In Hungary, piecemeal reforms have been going on for 22 years. Moreover, its traditional openness towards the West has put Hungary in a privileged position in the East. In contrast to the USSR, liberalization in the agricultural sector has guaranteed a sufficient supply of food. However, industrial reorganization is still in its initial stage. In early 1991, more than 80 per cent of all prices were free. But a lack of competitiveness in the state sector is obvious, and state-owned companies continue to rely heavily on subsidies. The government will have to make great efforts to enforce privatization and cut industry subsidies. The foreign debt burden of about US$ 20 billion has to be coped with. The trade surplus achieved in the first half of 1990 could be increased if the country had access to the

European agricultural market. The high internal debt has fueled inflation (at 28 per cent in 1990) and driven interest rates to a figure of 33 per cent and more, and the budget deficit has to be reduced. Nevertheless, one can count on a high level of entrepreneurship because of a well preserved private enterprise tradition. By early 1991, 20 per cent of the economy was in private hands and almost 2500 joint ventures had been arranged.

Czechoslovakia has attempted to establish part of the institutional infrastructure first. It has one of the most advanced industries of the ex-Comecon countries, the industrial sector accounting for 60 per cent of the country's GDP, and was one of the leading industrial countries before the communist take-over in 1948. Fading intra-Comecon trading relations must soon be replaced by a role in the international division of labour. For example, two-fifths of all exports used to go to the USSR in exchange for oil imports. This kind of trade has broken down almost completely. The 'small privatization' has started in Czechoslovakia: retail stores, restaurants and smaller business units are put up for auction. The government will have to withdraw subsidies for non-competitive sectors. A reform programme aiming at price liberalization and currency convertibility for most current account transactions was implemented at the beginning of 1991. Resulting unemployment during the period of transition could well be substantial. In the long run, the geographical advantage of being located in the very centre of Europe may play an important role. The neighbouring markets of Austria and Germany will fuel export demand, thereby raising the level of employment.

In contrast to other Central and Eastern European countries, there is a complete lack of comprehensive reforms in the USSR. More importantly, there is no political consensus on the concept of reform. One fraction of the Communist Party still sticks to the idea of introducing market elements into the socialist system to arrive at a so-called 'socialist market'. This group does not accept private property. But working out a concept for a third way will be in vain. Another group favours the Javlinsky–Shatalin plan, which regards private property as the fundament of a promising reform strategy. According to this '500 days plan', agricultural cooperatives must be decentralized and privatized immediately to avoid food shortages or even famine. Shatalin advocates privatization and price deregulation at the same time. Unfortunately, the Shatalin programme has been rejected by the central government. It will take a decade or more to reform the extremely distorted industrial structure.

When discussing reforms with economists from the Soviet Union, one gets the impression that even intellectuals only think in terms of partial or half-way reforms:

1 There is no freeing of prices at one stroke, and 'price reform' is misinterpreted as the correction of distorted prices in the right direction. Artificially low prices are raised, but there still will be a cap on prices, implying that distortions will continue.
2 The system of central planning has not yet been abandoned. Output and input quantities are still communicated to firms, even though only for 60–70 per cent of output, with the remaining percentage being allocated by the corrected prices. In effect, the coexistence of quantitative and price allocation implies serious inconsistencies, giving rise to an allocational vacuum.
3 There is no clear-cut introduction of property rights, only a tentative attempt with hybrid forms of property rights.
4 There is no opening to the world market, only some modification of the preferred autarchy position.

This half-hearted approach to transition will not succeed. In addition to the lack of a promising concept for the transformation, the issues of distribution of political power, tax revenue, expenditure and property rights to natural resources and state firms, let alone of the Union and the Republics, are still undecided.

4

The Economic Integration
of Germany

4.1 A Special Case of the Transformation of a Socialist Economy

The economic and political integration of what is now called post-wall Germany has been proceeding with tremendous speed. In November 1989, the time horizon was a ten-year period with two independent states slowly adjusting to each other. In January 1990, the time horizon was down to three years; two currencies and a flexible exchange rate as a shock absorber for East German industry were still discussed. By early 1991, some important aspects of integration had already been completed. In the silent revolution in Eastern Germany and in the process of integration, economic ideas and concepts depreciated very quickly. As someone said during the demonstrations in Leipzig: 'The word ages in your mouth'.

As was argued in chapter 3, there are three major areas of reform in the transition of socialist economies: establishing the institutional infrastructure, providing monetary stability and adjusting the real economy, especially at the micro-level, in the area of firms. In the German case, two of these problems are already basically solved. The institutional infrastructure was created by adoption of the West German economic system, including the constitution. Monetary stability was provided by the monetary union of 1 July 1990. Conversion of the East German Mark to the Deutschmark went surprisingly smoothly. So the problem to be solved is the real adjustment of the East German economy.

Germany is a special case of the transition of a socialist economy. The German experience can only shed light on the adjustment issue. At the same time, the political conditions that allowed a new institutional infrastructure and monetary stability to be reached quickly established other specifics for the German case, such as the migration of people, the non-availability of the exchange rate to serve as a shock absorber, the wage-setting process under the influence of the Western German wage level and the problems of establishing ownership.

What are the prospects of adjustment? Do the long-run prospects differ from the short-run phenomena? How high will unemployment be in Eastern Germany? What size of transfers from Western to Eastern Germany will be needed? Will fiscal stability be affected by these transfers? Will we have a conflict between fiscal policy on the one hand and monetary policy on the other hand? What are the international implications?

4.2 The Long-run Effects

In the medium run of four to five years and especially in the longer run German economic integration will be an economic success, for three reasons: the integration effect, the capital accumulation effect and the changed economic system (Siebert, 1990c).

The Integration Effect

From an allocation point of view, the economic integration of Germany can be seen as the integration of two economies that have different factor endowments and that are at different levels of development; more specifically, economic integration can be interpreted as adding qualified labour, land and a partially obsolete capital stock to the West German economy. Eventually, the capital stock per worker in the area of Eastern Germany will reach the West German level and the economic structure will tend to equalize. We know that merging two economies with different endowments implies integration gains.

The sector structure of Eastern Germany was distorted towards agriculture and manufacturing and biased against services; 40.2 per cent of employment was in manufacturing and the producing crafts, whereas this figure was 33.6 per cent in Western Germany. While the Federal Republic has reduced employment in manufacturing from 10

(1970) to 8 million (1989), Eastern Germany has increased it from 2.9 to 3.4 million. The trade structure of Eastern Germany was distorted too. According to the old GDR statistics, in 1988, 69.4 per cent of Eastern Germany's exports went to the Comecon countries (4.5 per cent for Western Germany). This is the result of the intra-bloc specialization philosophy of Comecon. Moreover, Eastern Germany followed an import substitution strategy, aiming at a kind of autarky and an industrial base similar to that of Western Germany. It attempted to produce the product set of the world economy. The export share in GNP of Eastern Germany is estimated at 25 per cent. This is low for a small open economy. If the international division of labour had played freely, Eastern Germany should have had an export share in the range of 50 per cent, like that of countries of comparable size such as the Netherlands. This gap in export shares indicates the magnitude of the transformation of the economy that has to be performed. The gap also indicates the tremendous gains from trade that Eastern Germany did not realize in the past.

The area of the former GDR will experience a process of structural change similar to that of other European countries, but with less time for adjustments. Ailing industries, no longer competitive in international markets, such as shipbuilding, to some extent steel and textiles, will be a problem. Pollution- and energy-intensive sectors will have to adjust. New products satisfying international demand will have to be developed. The underdeveloped service sector will expand considerably. The size of the structural adjustment needed is aggravated by the distortions arising from central planning.

The integration effect in Germany is similar to the integration effect in Western Europe. The Delors initiative of Europe 1992 has stimulated the old continent, and we expect gains from integration in Western Europe. And we have observed that firms prepare for Europe 1992 with investments as well as with mergers and acquisitions. German integration is a Europe 1992 between the Rhine and the Oder.

The Capital Accumulation Effect

Growth theory predicts and historical experience confirms that a country similar in technical skills and technology to other countries, but starting out with a relatively low capital stock per head, will have a lower output initially but high growth rates. Countries which had their capital stocks partly destroyed in the Second World War,[1] or countries with a low capital stock relative to the inflow of refugees (12 million in the case of Germany), experienced high growth rates (Germany 7.5 per cent, Italy 5.7 per cent, Japan 8.1 per cent in 1950–60). High growth rates went along with a high investment ratio. On the other hand, countries with a capital endowment not affected by the war had lower growth rates (United States 3.2 per cent, United Kingdom 2.6 per cent) and a lower investment ratio.

The capital stock of East German industry is largely obsolete, for a number of reasons. First, the capital goods (equipment and buildings) are old: 54.9 per cent of equipment in industry is older than 10 years. The capital stock is geared towards distorted environmental and energy costs. Moreover, production and the capital stock were oriented to Comecon, an external market with many distortions; hence many products cannot compete internationally because of their poor quality. Eastern Germany, with an obsolete capital stock, will experience an investment boom – this implies positive growth prospects.

Incentives

The move from a centrally planned economy with government ownership of the means of production to a market economy will increase economic efficiency. The motivation of people will change. This holds for workers, for whom pay and effort will be more closely related, as well as for entrepreneurs, who were non-existent before. Profits will be a strong incentive to improvement of the allocation of resources and to innovation. Economic decisions will be delegated to the market and will be de-politicized, so that efficiency will increase. Markets will allow gains from internal specialization; for instance, markets deliver products at the right time (and the right place), so that large inventories are no longer necessary and idleness of labour can be prevented.

---

[1] The extent to which the capital stock of Germany was destroyed by the war is debated (Gundlach, 1987; Schmieding, 1990).

4.3 The Difference from 1948

With these positive medium- and long-run prospects, which are
sometimes doubted in Germany, why do we not observe an economic
miracle in Eastern Germany right away (Siebert, 1991)?

After the economic and monetary reform of 1948 in Western
Germany the index of industrial production rose by 50 per cent in the
first five months (Wallich, 1955, p. 33), and annual growth rates of
real GNP reached 20 per cent in 1949–51.[2] In principle, the situation
in Eastern Germany is comparable to Western Germany's in 1948,
because in both cases we see a rich pool of qualified labour and a
capital shortage, in 1948 because the capital stock was partly
destroyed by the war and because additional capital accumulation was
necessary to equip 12 million refugees, now because the capital stock
of Eastern Germany is obsolete in economic and ecological terms.
Nevertheless, there are marked differences between 1948 in Western
Germany and the situation in Eastern Germany now. These
differences relate to the inefficiency of firms, the J-curve of output
and employment, ownership uncertainty, the wage-setting process
and the political economy of transition.

Inefficiency of Firms

Most Eastern German firms are inefficient; they are the product of
the socialist central planning approach. The obsoleteness of the
capital stock of the economy finds its expression in the inefficiency of
firms. In the production of the Trabant, IFA, the East German car
manufacturer, employed 65,000 people to produce 200,000 cars per
year. Toyota, with the same employment, produces 4,000,000 per
year, a productivity ratio of 1:20. In general, East German productivity in
March 1990 was estimated at one-third of the West German level.
Firms were state monopolies, comprising the whole industry. They
were not exposed to competition, either from potential producers at
home because of the demarcation of markets or from producers

[2] GNP growth rates in Western Germany (at constant 1936 prices) were: 1949,
second half-year 18.7 per cent; 1950, first half-year 13.5 per cent; second half-year
19.6 per cent; 1951, first half-year 20.6 per cent; second half-year 9.5 per cent. Data
are not available for before 1949 (Wallich, 1955, p. 34).

abroad because of the philosophy of specialization in Comecon. Moreover, prices, including the system of industry or firm-specific exchange rates, were distorted.

The inefficiency of existing firms is a starting condition different from that of 1948. You first have to dismantle the old structures. In 1948 one could start from scratch or adjust intact production processes to the new economic conditions. Moreover, in 1948 some adjustment had already taken place in Western Germany, with industrial output already rising from 1945 to 1948.

The J-Curve of Output

As explained in chapter 3, the transition of a socialist planned economy to a market economy will follow a J-curve where, in the transitional period, industrial output and GNP will fall. Existing firms are not competitive for a number of reasons, and the transition from a centrally planned economy will bring to light the veiled distortions and inefficiencies in this economy. Unemployment, although it did not officially exist, was hidden and will now become apparent. It will take time for new firms to come into existence. Such a J-curve of output and u-curve of employment will hold for all economies in transition from a planned system to a market economy (see figures 3.2 and 3.3). Industrial output was 50 per cent lower in August 1990 than in August 1989.

Uncertainty of Property Rights

A specific problem of transition in Germany is ownership uncertainty. As a basic principle, all owners who were dispossessed after 1949 will be reinstated as owners. However, where the land has been used for buildings, reinstating the previous owners may not be possible. Compensation will have to be paid. Compensation will also be required when investment has taken place. If the market value of a lot and the compensation rate differ too much, there is a strong incentive to go to the courts. This creates uncertainty for investment. Moreover, property rights are uncertain because no clear records of titles exist. Expropriations between 1945 and 1949 under the military Russian government will not be undone, as was recently confirmed by the Constitutional Court.

As of March 1991, a recorded claim by a previous owner froze the sale of a firm. This impeded privatization by Treuhand or even made it impossible. It was not uncommon for 30 claims to be put on a specific firm because an existing firm is a combination of many previous properties.

The basic problem is that ownership of land and firms has to be established in an administrative process. Administrative decisions can be questioned in court, and court battles may very well take half a decade. Since property rights uncertainty deters investment, an arrangement must be found that reduces uncertainty. One possibility is to reduce the wedge between the market value of a piece of land when the owner is reinstituted and the compensation rate by paying compensation near the market value. Another approach is to attach less weight to the previous owner and to give priority to the quick definition of property titles, including the establishment of new owners, if in this way new firms are quickly introduced and investment picks up. This is attempted in a new legal approach giving preference to employment and investment.

The Wage-setting Process

Another difference from 1948 is the application of West German labour regulations to the East, the impact of the Western German wage level on the wage-setting process and the relationship of the wage-setting process to competitiveness. In 1949 the Deutschmark was devalued by 20 per cent, whereas the conversion of the Ost-Mark represented an appreciation. With the exchange rate no longer available to improve the competitiveness of East German firms, in principle the wage rate should take over the function of giving Eastern Germany a temporary comparative advantage in labour-intensive industries. However, one has to recognize some mechanisms that reduce the wage differential. Since highly skilled workers are rather mobile, their wages cannot differ too much between Eastern and Western Germany. This is not an argument in favour of the same wage rate for *all* types of labour in Eastern and Western Germany but an argument for a differentiation of the wage structure in Eastern Germany. Highly qualified and mobile labour must earn the same wage as in Western Germany. Commuters near the previous border will raise the wage rate in the western parts of the former GDR; this also holds for Berlin. Firms in the service sector in Eastern Germany, such as banks and insurance companies, seem to pay the same wages to employees regardless of whether they come from Eastern Germany or Western Germany. Finally, trade unions will push for high wage increases. Thus, a favourable labour endowment at low wages provides only a temporary comparative advantage. In the transition period, there is a risk that wages will increase more than productivity and that additional unemployment will be created by the wage rate. However, it should be recognized that the ex-GDR has a qualified stock of labour, which implies a comparative advantage due to the availability of skilled labour in the long run. Moreover, the movement of labour to Western Germany puts downwards pressure on wage increase in Western Germany in the transitional period. The additional supply of labour through commuters and immigration should limit wage increases in Western Germany.

The Market versus the Political Process

Another caveat to the optimistic long-run growth scenario described above should be mentioned. There is a risk that real economic adjustment in the integration of the two Germanies will not be brought about by market forces but by the political process. There is no doubt that it was the role of the political process to define institutional integration, such as the negotiation of the treaty between the two Germanies. However, real economic integration should be brought about by market forces. In the case of converting the two currencies and wages, the political process has not relied on market forces to determine the conversion rate for currencies or to find the equilibrium wage, including the equilibrium wage structure. There is a definite risk that the political process will dominate the privatization of firms and sectoral adjustment. Moreover, there is a strong political demand for structural protection of Eastern German industry, for a slowed adjustment process and for other types of intervention.

The aspirations of the inhabitants of the ex-GDR are high, resulting in a political demand for quick improvements in income, environmental quality, housing, social security and physical infrastructure. There seems to be a belief that government policy can solve these issues quickly. In this respect, the analogy to 1948 no longer holds. If these political demands are allowed to influence the course of events and if they dominate the market process, prices will be politicized. In this case, structural change in Eastern Germany will take place along similar lines to Western Germany's experience, with a sectoral policy for ailing industries. There will then be a risk of the GDR turning into a *Ruhrgebiet* or a *mezzogiornio* and, consequently, no reason for optimism.

4.4 Restructuring Industry, Privatization, Bottlenecks

Some of the specific issues of the transition relate to the restructuring of industries, privatization and specific bottlenecks.

The Restructuring of Industry

The core of the adjustment process of socialist economies is the restructuring of industry, as explained in chapter 3. Industry and services in the GDR were organized into 321 vertically and horizontally integrated *Kombinats*. Of these, 126 industrial *Kombinats* were directly controlled by the central branch ministries and the remainder (95 industrial) by regional authorities. The *Kombinat* encompassed essentially the whole industrial branch, with a clearly segmented market. The *Kombinat* was protected against internal competition by governmental demarcation of markets; it was protected against competition from abroad by the philosophy of international specialization.

As in the transformation of industry in any socialist country, in the restructuring of the existing forms three different aspects have to be distinguished: (1) legal independence, (2) the economic efficiency of organizational units and (3) ownership. By law, all existing firms (roughly 8000) have been declared legally independent. Thus, in a legal sense, the *Kombinat* has already been broken up to some extent into sub-units. However, the problem of creating an efficient organizational unit that can survive in the market is not yet solved. Thus, the existing units – there are 40,000 organizational units or plants (*Betriebsstätten*) – have to be restructured by the elimination of the production of intermediate inputs that can be provided more cheaply by markets and by the removal of inefficient repair departments.

The organizational restructuring of firms is linked to the issue of privatization. All state firms are now owned by the Treuhandanstalt, a government trust agency. The role of Treuhand is to privatize the firms and eventually to return the proceeds obtained from privatization to the government. Thus, Treuhand should have a limited existence. However, Treuhand may be tempted to make firms efficient in order to find a buyer or receive a better price. Moreover, there is a strong political demand that Treuhand should undertake structural policy, eventually releasing potentially viable firms to the free market. Thus, there is a risk that Treuhand will become a super 'machinery' of sectoral policy that will be exposed to strong pressure in the political process. It is quite clear that Treuhand cannot successfully undertake structural policy. Such an approach would repeat the mistakes of central planning, and it would fail.

In order to prevent such an outcome, Treuhand should not be allowed to invest in new projects or to use receipts from privatization to alleviate the adjustment process of ailing firms. Otherwise financial resources would be wasted. Moreover, an institutional mechanism should be developed by which individual firms can dissociate themselves from Treuhand, for instance by pointing out a potential investor. Potential investors should also be given the right to initiate the privatization. Treuhand could then be forced to give its consent to the privatization of a firm within a prescribed period, such as two months. An auction should be used as a safeguard against the sale of a firm at too low a price. By means of such institutional arrangements, one could make sure that Treuhand eventually disappeared. Moreover, Treuhand should place priority on quick privatization because privatization is a precondition for investment and employment to pick up. If privatization takes time, investment will not come.

New Firms

The reorganization of existing firms is only one aspect of the restructuring of the East German economy. Restructuring must also come about through the establishment of new firms, especially new small firms. The new firms must create new jobs in order to absorb employees laid off as a result of the restructuring of inefficient existing firms. It is worth remembering that in Western Germany's manufacturing and mining sector (*gewerbliche Wirtschaft*) 78 per cent of jobs are in firms with less than 500 employees. In Eastern Germany this share is much lower (15 per cent, with 73.2 per cent of employment in firms with more than 1000 employees).

Specific Difficulties

There are specific difficulties and bottlenecks that determine the initial situation in the task of transforming the GDR economy into a market economy.

1   Environmental vintage damage. The costs of cleaning up soil contamination and other vintage damages make a potential investment less attractive. The polluter-pays principle cannot be applied; the government has to take over these burdens.

2   Infrastructure. Roads, the railway system, airports and the telecommunication system are deficient. They represent important bottlenecks for economic development. It is like driving on an *Autobahn*, hitting a repair section and getting into stop-and-go traffic or a complete stop. None of the dynamic forces can move because of a bottleneck.

3   Location space. A very important example of a bottleneck in infrastructure is the non-availability of location space. Location space is an important condition of entry for new firms, especially for the small firms that will create the necessary jobs. If location space is not available, the old existing firms will have a location advantage relative to potential newcomers. I have therefore proposed that location sites should be developed not by the government but by private initiative after the government has taken a basic decision on land use. This would have the advantage that location space would be provided much more quickly; moreover, infrastructure could be financed from private sources.

4.5 The Macroeconomic Outlook

I have contrasted the long-run positive outlook with the transition problems, especially with real adjustment in firms. Clearly, the adjustment of firms will have macroeconomic implications, as stressed in the J-curve of adjustment. Thus, the transition has also important short-run macroeconomic aspects.

Split Business Cycle

There is a split business cycle between Western and Eastern Germany. East Germans seem to favour West German products. Thus, aggregate demand for West German products increases, creating additional demand and adding one percentage point to Western Germany's real growth rate of 4.6 per cent in 1990. Because of a lack of demand for East German goods, there is a depression in the East. Employment is falling, and up to 3 million short-time workers and unemployed are expected for 1991. There is thus a split business cycle situation (Boss et al., 1990). Because of monetary union, monetary policy is no longer in a position to differentiate between the business cycle situations in the two Germanies.

Transfers and Budget Deficit

Government transfers from Western to Eastern Germany will be needed for quite a few purposes: for building up the social overhead capital in the GDR; for improving the environmental situation, especially for cleaning up past damage; for contributing to the social security system in the transitional phase; for financing the budget deficits of the Eastern German states; for honouring long-run contracts with the Russians; for financing the potential losses of Treuhand; and, possibly, for alleviating structural problems resulting from the lack of competitiveness of GDR industry and agriculture. In addition, foreign debt had to be taken over.

The overall German budget deficit (federal state, states, districts, communes) for 1991 is estimated to be 140 billion DM. This amounts to roughly 5 per cent of GNP (Boss et al., 1990). It is quite clear that a deficit in the neighbourhood of 5 per cent of GNP cannot be upheld for a series of years. Western Germany had a similar ratio in 1975 (5.7 per cent) and 1982 (4.1 per cent). In these two years there was not a positive prospect of growth, as can be expected in Eastern Germany. The political process has not been vigorous enough to reduce expenditure and to find innovative methods of financing.

1 Government expenditures are being cut only slightly. Over time regional subsidies for Berlin and the former border regions will be reduced; for instance, workers and firms in West Berlin still have

tax privileges. These so-called costs of the division of Germany
have been estimated at 40 billion DM per year.
2 Subsidies in Western Germany have been estimated by the Kiel
Institute of World Economics (Klodt, Schmidt et al., 1989) to
amount to 130 billion DM per year. Subsidies have not been
seriously attacked.
3 Financing public infrastructure privately would have had the
advantage of not relying on the governmental decision process and
so providing infrastructure in Eastern Germany quickly. However,
there was not too much practical experience with privatizing the
infrastructure; thus, German polity was not ready for this option.
4 Privatizing public property in Western Germany was only briefly
discussed as an additional possibility. Some firms are still totally or
partly owned by the federal government, such as Lufthansa and
Salzgitter; the *Länder* and the municipalities own quite a few firms
including the savings and loans banks.

This may have been the time to restructure the German tax system.
There are some basic points in the revision of any tax system. Taxing
capital is extremely difficult because capital is mobile. Thus, if taxes
are unfavourable to capital, capital will leave the country and the
country may shoot itself in the foot. The alternative would be to tax
immobile factors of production, such as labour, but this implies that
the substitution between work and leisure is affected and that effort is
reduced. Thus, a government does not have many options for taxing
capital and labour, especially if it wants to keep a business cycle
expansion going. However, it might be a good idea to introduce
economic incentives in the environmental area by charging for
emissions. So one would have liked to see a revision of the tax system,
innovative methods of financing and a reduction in government
spending, including subsidies. But such an option would have
required time. The government has decided differently, raising
contributions to unemployment insurance (paid by employers and
employees), the gas tax, and putting a surcharge on income, including
corporate income.

Fiscal Expansion versus Monetary Restraint

There is strong political pressure for an increase in government
expenditure in the transitional period. This implies a demand

stimulus and an expansionary fiscal policy. With transfers being largely financed by bonds, there is pressure for the interest rate to rise from the demand side, in addition to a supply-side increase in the rate of return. Such an expansionary fiscal policy limits the manoeuvring space of the Bundesbank, and monetary policy may very well have to be restrictive to maintain price level stability. Thus the economic policy situation is similar to that in the United States in the early 1980s, and we may see a conflict between an expansionary fiscal policy and monetary restraint.

4.6 International Implications

In American economic literature there is the concept of the 'new frontier' (first mentioned by Alvin Hansen, according to Higgins (1968)), a concept that derives from American historical experience of the expansion of the economic space over the Mississippi and beyond the Rockies, and that was extended to outer space by John F. Kennedy. German unification is such a new frontier. The paradigm to be applied to this investment scenario can be attributed not to Keynes but to Schumpeter. The huge productivity gap between Western and Eastern Germany signals potential productivity gains. The real rate of return will rise, and German unification will be a positive supply shock for Europe and the world economy.

Capital Flows and the German Current Account

Private capital will flow into Eastern Germany. There will also be public transfers from the West to the East. Capital exports from Western Germany, which amounted to 118 billion DM in 1989 (120 billion DM in 1988), will be reduced. Moreover, capital flows in Europe will be shifted to the German union in the transitional period. It can be expected that the real interest rate will be driven up because the marginal efficiency of capital in Eastern Germany has increased and new investment opportunities are opening up. Moreover, financing of the government budget deficit through bonds will raise the interest rate. This implies that borrowing will become more expensive elsewhere in the world.

There is a high real interest rate in Germany relative to the USA and there has been an increase in the real rate in Germany in 1989 and again in the middle of 1990. The difference from the real interest rate in the USA was widening at the end of 1990 (figure 4.1). In figure 4.1, the *ex post* interest rate is used. The alternative approach would apply the *ex ante* real interest rate, which is defined as the *ex ante* nominal interest rate and inflationary expectations, i.e. expected changes in the inflation rate. Actual nominal long-term interest rates reflect both the expected nominal interest rate and the expected inflation rate. Unfortunately, proxies for inflationary expectations are not available. Nominal long-term interest rates show an increase for Germany (see figure 4.2), especially after announcement of the monetary union on 7 February 1991. The difference between US and German nominal interest rates disappears, and even becomes negative. The difference between French and German nominal interest rates becomes positive (figure 4.2).

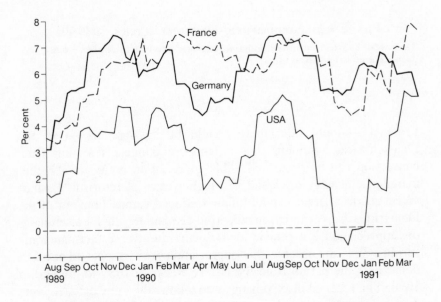

Figure 4.1   Real long-term interest rates, 1989–91.

The real long-term interest rate is defined as the difference between the interest rate of long-term government bonds and the rate of change of the consumer price index (three-month average).
Source: The *Economist*, various issues

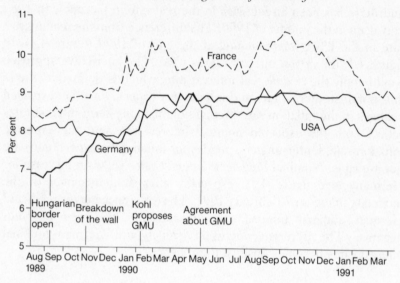

Figure 4.2   Nominal long-term interest rates, 1989–91.

The nominal long-term interest rate is the interest rate of long-term government bonds.
Source: The *Economist*, various issues

Exchange Rate Effects

From the supply side, there should be an appreciation of the Deutschmark, assuming that inflationary dangers resulting from conversion can be prevented. This appreciation is due to a higher marginal efficiency of capital, i.e. higher rates of return in Eastern Germany, to a larger capital inflow (reduced capital flow out of the Deutschmark area) and to an increased demand for the Deutschmark; the appreciation is a vehicle for reducing the overall German trade surplus. We can observe this appreciation with respect to the US dollar over the period from the last 12 weeks of 1989 to the end of 1990. The ECU–dollar exchange rate follows the same pattern. Note that investment prospects in Germany are only one side of the picture. The depreciation of the dollar is needed to generate a decrease in the US trade deficit (figure 4.3).

Eastern Germany, being a net importer of capital in the transitional period, will have a balance of trade deficit. The East German trade

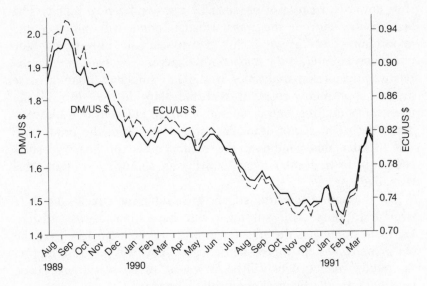

Figure 4.3 Exchange rates, 1989–91 (weekly averages).

Source: Deutsche Bundesbank, *Blick durch die Wirtschaft*, weekly

deficit will be caused by the import of investment goods, but it will also stem from the import of consumption goods. Eastern Germany's negative trade balance implies that the overall German trade surplus and German capital exports will be reduced. This impact can already be observed. In 1990, Germany's current account surplus was 32.1 billion DM lower than in 1989. In the third quarter of 1990, Germany's imports surged, for instance by 15 per cent from the EC (15.1 per cent from France, 16.0 per cent from Italy), whereas exports stagnated (−0.3 per cent).

The Deutschmark will appreciate in the context of tradeables and non-tradeables as well. In such a context the price for tradeables will be given by the world market; the price for non-tradeables will rise for a number of reasons: income transfer to Eastern Germany, supply-side growth leading to an increase in income, and infrastructure outlays in Eastern Germany will all increase the demand for non-tradeables. All these forces will raise internal absorption. Moreover, wages and consequently production costs for non-tradeables will rise; price controls on non-tradeables will be lifted. At the same time, the transformation function between tradeables and non-tradeables will shift upwards because of productivity gains and capital inflow. The bias in the shift in the transformation curve will influence the opportunity costs of producing non-tradeables. This supply-side effect may counteract the impact of the increase in absorption on the relative price of non-tradeables. It would be sufficient for an increase in the opportunity costs of non-tradeables if the shift in the transformation function was neutral or biased in favour of tradeables. Then the price of non-tradeables would rise from the production side. Under this condition, the relative price of non-tradeables compared to tradeables rises, implying an appreciation of the real exchange rate.

An alternative scenario comes to a different conclusion. If a structural policy with subsidies and huge transfers to Eastern Germany dominates the adjustment process, the inefficiencies of the old planning system will be perpetuated. This will put a burden on the public budget, debt will be increased, or taxes will have to be raised. Then, the Deutschmark will depreciate.

In the scenario for an appreciation of the Deutschmark, there will be pressure on the EMS for a re-alignment. Without re-alignment, the EMS countries will experience an increase in the interest rate. This pressure for re-alignment will arise from forces in the real economy, such as supply-side income growth, increased internal absorption and capital inflow into Germany. Moreover, the ECU is appreciating relative to the dollar, thus contributing to a reduction in the imbalance of the current account of the United States, at the same time making it harder for European countries to remain competitive. This will be an additional pressure for re-alignment in the EMS. Admittedly, these pressures for re-alignment will be (partly?) offset by increased German import demand for European products.

Germany should be more deeply integrated into the EC. At the moment, there is a great preparedness in all political parties in Germany to cede political power to the European parliament, and Germany's neighbours should grasp this opportunity. Of course, as an economist, one would like to see an institutional arrangement in Europe in which competition prevails, markets are open, Europe does not close itself off from the world and monetary stability is satisfied.

5

Europe in the World Economy

5.1 The Beauty Contest between Eastern Europe, Latin America and Asia

While Eastern European countries cope with the process of transition, they will compete against each other in the market for foreign investment. Again, the concept of institutional competition applies. Those countries that succeed best in redesigning their economic systems will attract the greatest share of capital inflow and new technology. For this reason, the countries are not completely independent when deciding on changes in their institutional structure. Any step away from opening markets, establishing private ownership and freeing prices will be punished by a withholding of foreign funds that otherwise would have come. Furthermore, as soon as monetary reforms provide a stable and convertible currency, any policy switch will be reflected by the reaction of domestic capital owners. To avoid an exodus of capital, reforms have to be credible, decisive, massive and rapid.

The principle of institutional competition, of course, extends to the labour force as well. The process of transition directly influences workers' expectations about their future. If people do not believe that steps towards a market economy are irreversible, a dramatic wave of emigration is likely to occur. Just like governments in the common market of 'Europe 1992', Eastern European governments will be disciplined by the threat of factor movements to rival systems. To summarize the reasoning above, one cannot both open borders to foreign investment and hesitate to transform the economy at the same time. There is no doubt that this is true for any country, including the Soviet Union.

Those countries that successfully complete the basic reforms will find themselves more competitive in the world market, not only for goods but also for capital. There is a beauty contest in institutional infrastructures and incentive systems between Eastern Europe, Latin America and Asia. This may mean that capital moves away from developing countries to Eastern Europe, but it may also mean that developing countries will be more successful in attracting capital. The direction of capital flows depends on the result of institutional competition. In a free-trading world, with decreasing impediments to capital flows, countries remain in a permanent process of institutional competition. As was pointed out in chapter 2, this should lead to a superior performance by national governments with regard to the design of the institutional system, and hence a more efficient allocation of resources.

5.2 A New Paradigm for the World Economy

From an international point of view, the economic paradigm is changing for an important region of the world. Eastern Europe has experienced the Orwellian crisis of socialist ownership and central planning and the market economy has become the most attractive institutional arrangement for allocation. Compared to pure capitalism, the 'social market economy' may be appealing, with three important ingredients:

- economic power is controlled by open markets, competition and competition policy;
- social security is integrated into the economic system;
- environmental costs are internalized into the price mechanism – as a problem to be solved.

This change in the economic paradigm for an important region of the world has already radiated to the countries of Latin America and Africa, where markets will have a larger role in the future and government intervention will be pushed back. The intensified decentralization of the world economy and the increased role of markets provide better incentives, other motivations and more efficiency for the static allocation of resources as well as for innovations.

5.3 Integrating the New Market Economies into the European Economic Space

There is tremendous economic potential in Eastern Europe in terms of natural resources, land and labour, and a market with a population of 136 million in Bulgaria, Czechoslovakia, Hungary, Poland, Romania and Yugoslavia and 190 million in the European part of the USSR. However, the six Eastern European countries (not including the Soviet Union) produce an output equivalent to less than 10 per cent of the output of the European Community. 'The combined convertible currency exports of the seven countries [including the GDR] was only three-quarters of the exports of Hong Kong' (Institute of International Finance, 1990, p. 8). The convertible currency trade of those countries accounted for less than 40 per cent of their total trade.

So far, this economic potential has not been used. The region has had its own trade philosophy, attempting a specialization among Comecon by political coordination. Tractors would be produced in country x, railway carriages in country y, buses in country z. This was specialization from above, and was along the traditional Ricardian lines of Portuguese wine for English cloth and Russian oil for Czech machinery. Government contracts were the vehicle of specialization. Contrast this with a philosophy in which international trade develops from below, with a multitude of decentralized and individual contracts, and in which individual preferences play a role. Wine is exchanged for wine, a Peugeot for a BMW. A substantial part of the international trade of industrial countries is intra-industry trade. We can also compare the Eastern European trade philosophy of the self-sufficiency of Comecon with the export-orientation and openness of the successful Asian countries.

In an optimistic scenario, the economic reforms in Eastern Europe can represent a new frontier. The huge productivity gap between Western and Eastern Europe signals potential productivity gains. When the reforms succeed, there will be a positive supply shock for the world economy. The real rate of return will rise and capital will flow to Eastern Europe, where new production lines will open up. Eastern Europe has the potential to be a growth locomotive for the world economy in the 1990s. There is, as Bismarck would put it, a tremendous opportunity 'to seize history's coattails as he rushes by, or forever wait for the opportunity to return'. The optimistic picture of the liberalization process in Eastern Europe is dimmed by the clouds of centralization in the USSR, by its unwillingness or inability to introduce a federal structure and by its lack of a concept of reform. There is a definite risk that glasnost will go into reverse, and there is a risk that the instability of the USSR will externalize.

Economic reform in Eastern Europe must be a success. Just imagine the political implications of a failure: the market economy would have lost its credentials, and we might go back to an undemocratic, populist or authoritarian system. There is the risk of tremendous political instability. Some people are vexed by the idea that an economic disappointment in Eastern Europe will see a new wave of migration from the East to the West – a *Völkerwanderung*, a mass migration. Against such a mass movement of European dimensions, the German–German migration of 1989 and early 1990 would appear tiny.

Even if there is no political instability in Eastern Europe, there will be a poverty border along the Oder in five years when Eastern Germany has caught up. The ratio of income per capita between Western Germany (US$ 18,480) and Poland (US$ 1860) is 10:1 (World Bank, 1990b). There is already a poverty gradient along the Danube. With European borders no longer being equipped with machine guns, such income differences are not tenable. The situation is only sustainable if income per head in the East rises.

If Western Europe closes its markets to Eastern Europe – as in agriculture, textiles and other protected areas – the economic opportunities in Eastern Europe are dimmed; the incentive to emigrate will increase. There is an interdependence between protectionism and migration. This relation is especially relevant for German and Western European agricultural policy. Protecting Western European agriculture against the Australian or Brazilian farmer is different from protecting it against the Polish and Hungarian peasant. Whereas the Brazilian farmer cannot migrate to the EC, the Eastern European population of the countryside can. Thus, the protectionist politician will reap the harvest of his policy in immigration problems. Events in Eastern Europe have completely changed the conditions for agricultural policy in Europe in the future. The opportunity costs of protection will become apparent in migration.

It is an absolute necessity to open the EC to the countries of Eastern Europe, in some form or another. We can envision free trade agreements between the EC and individual countries, such as Poland, Czechoslovakia and Hungary, similar to the 1973 free trade agreement with EFTA in manufacturing. Conceivably, some Eastern European countries may form another economic union that will be associated with the EC. There can be looser forms of association with the Baltic states or other autonomous regions of the USSR, and possibly with Russia.

This European economic space can be viewed as a system of rings. The EC is the core, representing a region with fully integrated commodity and capital markets in which national regulations do not create market barriers because of the principle of institutional competition. Economic conditions and the standard of living are similar, with the periphery of Ireland, Portugal and Greece catching up. This ring will be enlarged by some EFTA countries explicitly joining the EC, among them perhaps Austria, Sweden and Norway. Possibly, inside the EC, some countries will be more intensely integrated in the area of monetary policy, but it can be expected that all EC countries will peg their currencies to the monetary anchor prevailing in the countries that are more intensely integrated in the monetary area.

Around the enlarged EC, there is a ring of countries that will be associated with the EC by a free trade agreement in which tariffs and quantitative restraints are reduced. This is a new EFTA for Poland, Czechoslovakia and Hungary, not only in manufacturing, it is hoped, but in agriculture as well. Finally, there is a ring of countries that will be less intensively integrated in the commodity markets, such as the Baltic states, regions of the USSR and Russia itself. Free enterprise zones, for instance for the Leningrad region or the Baltic states, can be more intensively integrated with the EC.

5.4 The Merit of Flexible Exchange Rates

In the monetary area, the European economic Space will consist of two different regions: a core European area with currencies linked to each other by more or less fixed exchange rates or even a common currency, and countries where exchange rates freely fluctuate against the currency of the core region. For the core region, comprising the Benelux countries, Denmark, France, Italy, Spain, the UK and Germany, there will be fixed exchange rates with capital mobility and a monetary anchor defining price level stability. Alternatively, a common currency may be established and the historical currencies may be given up. This, however, presupposes that a credible institutional arrangement for an autonomous European Central Bank steering the money supply is found. In either case, some members of the enlarged EC, not yet integrated monetarily, may follow the option of an exchange-rate oriented monetary policy, adjusting the money supply so that their currencies are *de facto* pegged to the anchor or the core currency. This was Austria's policy with respect to the Deutschmark in past years.

For the Eastern European countries, however, flexible exchange rates are needed. The integration of commodity markets by free trade arrangements does not imply a monetary union. On the contrary, the difference in the stage of development between Western and Eastern Europe and the necessary adjustment to Eastern European economies require a flexible exchange rate, both as a shock absorber and as a moderator of structural differences. A step in the right direction is to introduce convertibility of Eastern European currencies. Without 'internal' convertibility, prices will remain distorted, and monetary policy will not be credible. Without 'external' convertibility, foreign investment cannot be attracted. In the future, depreciation of Eastern European currencies may be an important vehicle on the road to economic integration. Of course, an individual Eastern European country has the option of pegging its currency to the Western European anchor and defending the chosen exchange rate. Then fiscal policy and incomes policy – and especially trade unions – have to adjust to this target. Alternatively, fixed exchange rates in Eastern Europe would require a transfer mechanism that – in comparison to the German case – has the characteristics of a nightmare.

5.5 The Protectionist Risk

The positive supply shock of Eastern Europe on the world economy is contingent on the stringency of reforms. The revitalization of Western Europe depends on whether the EC will be an open market for the rest of the world. How big is the risk of protectionism? Will the stimulating effects of institutional competition be eaten up by the efficiency losses from outside protection, anti-dumping, voluntary export restraints and structural policy? Is the stimulating effect of the single market only a dream in Delors country – a frenzy in Deloria? What are the stumbling blocks that might stop 1992 becoming a Schumpeterian event?

Institutional competition will abolish national regulations that in the past have benefited certain sectors or groups of an economy. Institutional competition and market entry will reduce rents, and thus the single market will meet with political opposition. With possibilities for protection and rent-seeking being reduced internally, there is a risk that external barriers to trade – to the extent that GATT obligations can be circumvented (e.g. Article 24) or already have been circumvented (e.g. Multifibre Agreement or other Voluntary Export Restraints) – will be made higher. Sectors being exposed to more contestable markets inside Europe may attempt to eliminate or reduce outside competition. Fortressphobia, which has been prevalent in the USA, sees the successors of the French fortress-builder Sebastian le Prestre de Vauban constructing walls, ramparts and moats. Ailing industries, such as shipbuilding, parts of the steel industry and coal, have been protected by a set of policy instruments, including subsidies. Here the political process – a strong coalition of firms, unions and politicians – may be tempted to establish outside protection at the European level. Finally, and importantly, agriculture that generates an excess supply that is dumped on the world markets has to be added to this picture.

National quantitative restrictions on imports from non-member states have been allowed by Article 115 of the Treaty of Rome. This implies a restriction of the flow of indirect imports from non-member countries coming through other EC countries. There are some 700 of these restrictions, relating to shoes, textiles, fresh bananas, television sets, motor cars and car radios. Five countries have more or less voluntary limits on Japanese car imports: Italy (1 per cent of new vehicle registration), France (3 per cent), Britain (10 per cent), Spain (1 per cent) and Portugal (percentage not available).

It can be expected that it will be tempting for the labour-rich countries in the European periphery, which are competing directly with the newly industrialized countries and other developing countries, to push for new trade barriers. These national quantitative restrictions on imports using Article 115 are not consistent with the Single Market;[1] the question is whether the national restrictions will be replaced by higher EC tariffs, by lower European quotas or by voluntary export restraints relating to Europe as a whole. The automobile industry is an important case in point. With national grandfather clauses not being consistent with a single market, there is strong political pressure for a ten-year grace period against Japanese car imports. This would represent a new CAP – a common automobile policy. There is no doubt that after such a protectionist period the Western European car industry would have become completely inefficient and incapable of competing in the world market.

Anti-dumping actions are proving to be an increasingly important means of keeping competition out or at least of reducing its impact. Of course, they can only be taken in accordance with the GATT rules and using the newly formulated EC Dumping Regulation (OJ, 2423/88). Based on evidence submitted by injured EC companies, the Commission must prove that a non-EC firm is selling its product in Europe at a lower price than at home. The foreign supplier then has to pay anti-dumping import duties or has to agree to raise the price in Europe (price undertaking). There have been about 100 complaints a year (*Economist*, 9 July 1989, p. 38), with proceedings initiated in about 50 cases and dumping being found in 30. There has been a noticeable increase since 1986 in the number of cases. According to Messerlin (1989), EC anti-dumping measures reduced imported quantities by 40 per cent in 1980–5, with an *ad valorem* equivalent of roughly 23 per cent.

Quantitative restraints at the European level as a substitute for national restraints (Article 115), anti-dumping and regional preferences (for instance, the free trade arrangement with EFTA) require local content rules. Moreover, a non-EC supplier may attempt to europeanize its product by producing the final stage in Europe ('screwdriver plant'). Rules of origin are the result of intervention in trade. Thus, one intervention implies the next. The basic definition of 1968 that goods originate where they undergo their 'last substantial transformation' has long been abandoned in specific cases by

---

[1] It should be underlined that Article 115 runs counter to one of the cornerstones of the setting up of a common market in the Treaty of Rome, namely the principle of free movement of goods laid down in Article 9.

excluding pure assembly, by requiring 'diffusion' for integrated circuits and by requiring percentages of value added (60 per cent for EFTA cars, 35–45 per cent for goods to be protected by Article 115, 80 per cent in the case of subsidies). Clearly, local content requirements are a severe blow to free trade in a world becoming more and more interdependent.

Strategic trade policy, a rediscovery by American economists of Friedrich List's idea of an early start or an early market entry, has been re-imported to Europe and has made an impact on some politicians in Europe. Of course, it has been long forgotten in the policy debate that the underlying oligopolistic models are naive, and that the results are not robust with respect to the assumptions. Moreover, the debate on strategic trade policy shows that its proponents have not understood the importance of incentives defined by the institutional setting of the market economy.

Politicians like their countries to be competitive in high-tech products, such as computers, chips and telecommunication equipment. A number of research programs have been launched (Eureka, Jessi, Esprit and the European Aero-Space Programme). The results of previous programmes that subsidized the development of nuclear plants or large computers have been disappointing, 'if not disastrous' (Trapp, 1989, p. 16). Politicians may be tempted to protect 'temporarily' the sectors they have chosen as promising, so as to justify their original choice. Finally, the European Commission is inclined to consider competition policy as being instrumental for strategic trade policy. Such a philosophy is certain to be a source of inefficiency in the long run.

5.6 A Plea for an Open Europe

When voicing these concerns, one should not forget that the EC is more open than North America or Japan. Taking the trade share[2] of GNP as an indicator for openness, the EC has a trade share of 9 per cent whereas North America has a share of 7.8 per cent and Japan a share of 6 per cent (table A6 in the appendix). According to some estimates, Article 115 relates to 3–4 per cent of community imports;

[2] Export share plus import share of GNP, divided by two.

anti-dumping actions relate to 1 per cent.[3] But these percentages may be so low because potential suppliers anticipate import restraints.

There is a risk that Western Europe will develop a protectionist tendency. This relates to European agricultural policy but also to sectors that, so far, have not been protected, such as the automobile sector, where national import quotas will be elevated on a European level. And there is a danger that the world economy will move away from multilateralism, and that the paradigm of bilateralism and the concept of a triad with strategic behaviour as dominant characteristic will take over.

It may be tempting to extend the principle of mutual recognition to the world as a whole, and to have the principle of mutual recognition as a cornerstone of the international economic order beside the most favoured nation clause. Whereas the most favoured nation clause is a vehicle to prevent discrimination in trade policy, the principle of mutual recognition is an institutional device to allow effective market access in a regulatory framework. But this approach seems to be too demanding. In the past ten years, reciprocity has become the keyword of economic diplomacy, relating both to trade barriers in the narrow sense and to the issue of market access in different national regulatory settings. The trade and access aspects overlap.

Some see the solution to protectionism in reciprocity. Of course, reciprocity as a bilateral balance in the value of trade is sheer nonsense; overall reciprocity is a wider concept meaning an opening up of countries without sector-by-sector matching. Sectoral reciprocity is a much more limited idea and follows the Roman principle of *do ut des* (give and you will receive) in liberalization sector by sector. In between are reciprocities on the treatment of firms, such as national treatment reciprocity, national treatment with effective access or equivalent treatment. Reciprocity may be instrumental in bringing about the liberalization of trade and a less restricted market access, but reciprocity may also prove to be a vehicle that will increase protectionism, reduce market access and destroy multilateralism. Thus, aggressive reciprocity may be used as a crowbar to open up markets. Although this sounds attractive, the crowbar has two ends, and the rear end may wreck the domestic economy, diverting resources from their best use, and initiating a devastating rent-

[3] Informal information from the Commission of the European Communities.

seeking process, which has brought many Latin American countries into poverty. We must prevent the experience of the 1930s, with beggar-thy-neighbour policies, successive rounds of depreciation and a vicious circle of protectionism.

An important issue is whether reciprocity will imply another orientation of international trade policy. The paradigm of the triad has become a powerful picture of the world, with North America having a GNP of US$ 5000 billion (and a population of 280 million), Europe a GNP of US$ 4200 billion in the EC (and a population of 340 million in the EC, 34 million in EFTA and 320 million in Eastern Europe) and the Pacific Rim a GNP of US$ 4000 billion (and a population of 1600 million). We become accustomed to thinking of the world in terms of regional blocks and we are not far from interpreting the international division of labour as a zero-sum game. This is the arena in which strategic trade policy flourishes, reciprocity is *en vogue* and regionalism wins over multilateralism. Unlike in the nineteenth century, when Great Britain, which was the hegemon, was clearly going for free trade, there is no dominating economic power that may lead the world to free trade.

It is somewhat ironic that the liberalization process in Eastern Europe should discover the merits of the free market, and give up the philosophy of planned specialization among countries by international political cooperation, at a time when Western Europe is tempted to close itself off in more areas and when new theoretical, albeit naive, approaches to international economics in the USA seem to suggest a new era of managed trade and harmonization of strategic trade policy. In the search for a policy orientation for the international community, we should not forget the failure of the entire continent of Latin America, which has based its economic policy in the past three decades on import-substitution and the protection of potential export sectors. And we should contrast this with the success stories of the East Asian countries that have followed an outward-oriented development strategy. Our aim must be to develop a multilateral institutional arrangement for the world economy in which economic decisions are decentralized and in which strategic or protectionist behaviour by individual countries or regions of the world is prevented by a credible commitment to the rules of the trade system.

Institutional and economic change in both Eastern and Western Europe is a tremendous opportunity for a positive change in the world economy. There is the chance of a larger economic space in Europe, and there are benefits from free trade for Western and far more for Eastern Europe. In addition, there is a peace dividend for both the West and the East, which allows a reduction in military expenditure and a redirection of expenditure to other uses. But most of all there is a freedom dividend for the people of Eastern Europe, who can now enjoy individual liberty. The world as a whole can benefit from the new momentum in Western Europe, if the EC remains open, and from integration of the Eastern European countries into the international division of labour. Europe can be a positive supply shock for the world economy and a growth stimulus. As David Hume once said: 'The increase of riches and commerce in any one nation, instead of hurting, commonly promotes the riches and commerce for all its neighbours.'

Appendix

Table A1 Value added tax rates in the EC, 1989

Country	Reduced rate	Normal rate	High rate
Belgium	1, 6, 17	19.0	25, 33
Denmark	–	22.0	–
FRG	7	14.0	–
France	2.1, 5.5, 13	18.6	25, 28
Greece	3, 6	16.0	36
Ireland	1.4, 5, 10	25.0	–
Italy	4, 9	19.0	38
Luxembourg	3, 6	12.0	–
Netherlands	6	18.5	–
Portugal	8	17.0	30
Spain	6	12.0	33
UK	–	15.0	–

Table A2 Number of mergers in the
Federal Republic of Germany, 1973–88

Year	Number of mergers
1973	34
1974	294
1975	445
1976	453
1977	554
1978	558
1979	602
1980	635
1981	618
1982	603
1983	506
1984	575
1985	709
1986	802
1987	887
1988	1150
1989	1450
1990	1500

Source: Report of the German Cartel Office on its activities
in the year 1987–8 and 1990

Table A3 Intra-EC investment

Country	Units[a]	Years[b]	Inward investment from Europe	(% of total inward investment)	Outward investment to Europe	(% of total outward investment)
Belgium	m BFr	1959–81	89,520	(37.5)	–	–
Denmark	m DKr	1974–83	6,636	(38.8)	5.680	(41.0)
France	m FFr	1975–83	49,056	(54.7)	29.443	(26.6)
FRG	m DM	1983	23,851	(29.6)	36.356	(34.3)
Greece	m US$	1953–78	387.8	(33.1)	–	–
Ireland	m IR£	1981	843.9	(37.3)	–	–
Italy	b L	1984	8,258	(45.8)	4.100	(29.1)
Netherlands	m NFl	1983	16,319	(31.5)	46.263	(38.6)
Portugal	m Esc	1983	22,639	(58.9)	–	–
Spain	b Pta	1960–83	410.21	(49.6)	61.73	(21.6)
UK	m £	1981	2,606.1	(15.4)	5,910.2	(20.7)

[a] m, million; b, billion. [b] Investment figures for single years represent capital stocks; investment figures for multiple-year periods represent cumulative investment flows.

Source: Giovannini and Hines, 1990, p. 59

Table A4   Main statutory corporate income tax rates

	1977	1989	Proposed or announced rate
EC countries			
Belgium	48	43	38
Denmark	37	50	35
France	50	39	34
Germany	56	56	50
Greece	39	46	–
Ireland	45	43	–
Italy	25	36	–
Luxembourg	40	34	–
Netherlands	48	35	–
Portugal	36	36.5	–
Spain	36	35	–
UK	52	35	–
GDP weighted average tax rates	47.21	42.08	39.08
Selected non EC countries			
Australia	50	39	–
Canada	46	42	–
Japan	40	42	37.5 (1990)
Sweden	56	52	30 (1991)
USA	48	34	–

Sources: Tanzi and Bovenberg, 1990; IMF International Financial Statistics; author's calculations

Table A5 Population, GNP, GNP per capita, GDP and GDP per capita in Middle and Eastern Europe, 1988

	Population (million)[b]	GNP (billion US$)[c]	GNP per capita (US$)	GDP (billion US$)[d]	GDP per capita (US$)[a]
Bulgaria	9.0	67.6	7 511	23.0	2 552
Czechoslovakia	15.6	158.2	6 000	66.3	4 246
GDR	16.4	207.2	12 634	203.6	12 388
Hungary	10.6	91.8	8 660	28.1	2 660
Poland	37.9	267.3	7 053	n.a.	n.a.
Romania	23.0	126.3	5 491	n.a.	n.a.
USSR	283.7	2535.3	8 937	1062.0	3 555
Yugoslavia	23.6	154.1	6 530	61.4	3 605
EC countries	324.3	4059.7	12 518		
FRG	78.0	870.0	14 192		
Spain	39.0	365.2	9 394		

n.a.: not available

[a] Converted from local currencies with end-of-year exchange rates.

Sources: [b] Stat. Bundesamt, 1990, and World Bank, 1990b; [c] CIA, 1989; [d] UN, 1989

Table A6 Exports and imports as share of GDP, 1970–88

| Year | EC[a] | | Japan | | USA | | North America (USA, Canada) | |
	Share of exports[b]	Share of imports[c]	Share of exports[b]	Share of imports	Share of exports[b]	Share of imports	Share of exports[b]	Share of imports
1970	9.0	9.1	9.5	9.3	4.2	4.0	3.6	3.0
1971	9.0	8.7	10.4	8.5	4.0	4.2	3.3	3.1
1972	8.5	8.4	9.3	7.7	4.0	4.6	3.2	3.5
1973	9.1	9.4	8.9	9.3	5.1	5.2	4.2	4.0
1974	11.2	12.6	12.1	13.5	6.5	6.9	5.4	5.5
1975	10.6	10.7	11.2	11.6	6.5	6.1	5.3	4.9
1976	10.8	11.9	12.0	11.5	6.3	6.9	5.1	5.4
1977	11.3	11.8	11.6	10.2	5.8	7.5	4.7	6.0

1978	10.8	10.9	10.0	8.1	6.1	7.7	5.0	6.2
1979	10.4	11.8	10.2	10.9	7.1	9.0	5.9	7.3
1980	10.6	13.0	12.3	13.2	7.9	9.5	6.9	7.8
1981	11.7	13.1	13.0	12.1	7.5	9.0	6.4	7.4
1982	11.5	12.7	12.8	12.0	6.6	8.1	5.7	6.5
1983	10.5	11.7	12.4	10.6	5.8	8.0	4.8	6.3
1984	11.4	12.6	13.6	10.7	5.8	9.1	4.6	7.2
1985	11.5	12.3	13.3	9.6	5.3	9.0	4.2	7.3
1986	9.7	9.6	10.7	6.5	5.4	9.3	4.2	7.6
1987	9.1	9.2	9.7	6.3	5.7	9.5	4.5	7.8
1988	n.a.	n.a.	9.3	6.6	6.7	9.5	5.3	7.8

n.a.: not available.
[a] Six countries 1970–1; nine countries 1972–9; ten countries 1980–2; twelve countries from 1983.
[b] Share of exports to third countries.
[c] Share of imports from third countries.

Source: OECD; GATT (various issues)

References and Bibliography

Birch, David (1984) The contribution of small enterprise to growth and employment. In Herbert Giersch (ed.), *New Opportunities for Entrepreneurship*. Symposium 1983, Kiel Institute of World Economics. Tübingen: J.C.B. Mohr (Paul Siebeck).

Bishop, Matthew R. and Kay, John A. (1989) Privatization in the United Kingdom: lessons from experience. *World Development*, 17 (5), 643–57.

Blanchard, Olivier and Layard, Richard (1990a) Privatising Eastern Europe: making it safe for capitalism. *Financial Times*, 11 July, 15.

—— and —— (1990b) Economic change in Poland. CEPR Discussion Paper no. 432, London.

Blue Ribbon Commission (1990) *Project Hungary – Action Programme for Hungary in Transformation to Freedom and Prosperity*. Budapest and Washington, DC: Blue Ribbon Commission.

Bobinski, Christopher and Wolf, Martin (1990) Radical options for privatization. *Financial Times*, 2 August.

Bofinger, Peter (1990) The role of monetary policy in the process of economic reform in Eastern Europe. CEPR Discussion Paper no. 457, London.

Boss, Alfred et al. (1990) Bundesrepublik Deutschland: Strukturelle Anpassungskrise im Osten – Hochkonjunktur im Westen. *Die Weltwirtschaft*, H. II, 25–42.

Brander, James and Spencer, Barbara (1985) Export subsidies and international market share rivalry. *Journal of International Economics*, 18, 83–100.

Burda, Michael and Gerlach, Stefan (1990) Exchange rate dynamics and currency unification: the Ostmark–DM rate. INSEAD Working Paper no. 90/78/EP, Fontainebleau.

Cecchini, Paolo, Catinat, M. and Jacquemin, A. (1988) *The European Challenge 1992: the Benefits of a Single Market*. Aldershot: Wildwood House.

CIA (various) *Handbook of Economic Statistics.* Washington, DC: CIA.

Collier, I.L. and Siebert, H. (1991) The economic integration of post-wall Germany. *American Economic Review (Papers and Proceedings),* Special Issue, May.

Commission of the European Community (1985) *Completing the Internal Market.* White Paper from the Commission to the European Council, Luxembourg.

Cook, Paul H. (ed.) (1988) *Privatization in Less Developed Countries.* New York: Harvester Wheatsheaf.

Cooper, Richard N. (1985) Economic interdependence and coordination of economic policies. In Ronald W. Jones and Peter B. Kenen (eds), *Handbook of International Economics, Vol. 2,* Amsterdam: North Holland, 1195–234.

De Grauwe, P. (1990) *The Economic Integration of West and East Germany. Two Tales Based on Trade Theory.* Leuven: CEPS and University of Leuven.

Dicke, Hugo (1989) Vollendung des EG-Binnenmarktes – der Versuch einer Zwischenbilanz. *Die Weltwirtschaft,* H. I, 88–111.

—— and Langhammer, Rolf J. (1990) The institutional framework and external dimension of the EC internal market. Kiel Institute of World Economics, Working Paper, no. 453.

Dornbusch, Rüdiger (1988) Notes on credibility and stabilization. NBER Working Paper no. 2790, Cambridge, MA.

Edwards, Sebastian (1989) On the sequencing of structural reforms. OECD, Department of Economics and Statistics, Working Paper no. 70, Paris.

—— and van Wijnbergen, Sweder (1986) The welfare effects of trade and capital market liberalization. *International Economic Review,* 27 (1), 141–8.

Emerson, M. (1988) *What a Model for Europe?* Cambridge, MA: MIT Press.

Emerson, M. et al. (1988) *The Economics of 1992. The EC Commission's Assessment of the Economic Effects of Completing the Internal Market.* Oxford: Oxford University Press.

Eucken, Walter (1952) *Grundsätze der Wirtschaftspolitik.* Tübingen: J.C.B. Mohr (Paul Siebeck).

Feldstein, Martin and Horioka, Charles (1980) Domestic saving and international capital flows. *Economic Journal,* 90, 314–29.

Frankel, Jeffrey (1989) Quantifying capital mobility. NBER Working Paper no. 2856, Cambridge, MA.

Frey, René L. (1977) *Zwischen Föderalismus und Zentralismus.* Frankfurt: Lang.

Giersch, Herbert (1985) Eurosclerosis. Kiel Institute of World Economics, Kiel Discussion Paper no. 112.

—— (1990) On being a public economist. Lecture held at the prize-awarding ceremony of the Paolo Baffi International Prize for Economics 1989, Kiel.

Giovannini, Alberto (1989) National tax systems versus the European capital market. *Economic Policy*, 4, 345–77.

—— and Hines, James R. Jr (1990) Capital flight and tax competition: are there viable solutions to both problems? CEPR Discussion Paper no. 416, London.

Grosfeld, Irena (1990) Prospects for privatization in Poland. *European Economy*, 43, 141–50.

Gundlach, Erich (1987) Währungsreform und wirtschaftliche Entwicklung: Westdeutschland 1948. Kiel Institute of World Economics, Kiel Working Paper no. 286.

Hayek, Friedrich A. von (1935) *Prices and Production*, 2nd edn. London: Routledge.

—— (1968) *Der Wettbewerb als Entdeckungsverfahren*. Kiel Institute of World Economics, Kieler Vorträge, N.F., no. 56. Tübingen: J.C.B. Mohr (Paul Siebeck).

—— (1977) *Entnationalisierung des Geldes, eine Analyse der Theorie und Praxis konkurrierender Umlaufsmittel*. Tübingen: J.C.B. Mohr (Paul Siebeck).

Heitger, Bernhard (1990) Wirtschaftliches Wachstum in Ost und West im internationalen Vergleich seit 1950. *Die Weltwirtschaft*, H. I, 173–92.

Hiemenz, Ulrich and Langhammer, Rolf J. (1989) Liberalization and the successful integration of developing countries into the world economy. In G.T. Renshaw (ed.), *Market Liberalization, Equity and Development*. Geneva: International Labour Office, World Employment Programme, 105–39.

Higgins, Benjamin J. (1968) *Economic Development. Principles, Problems and Policies*, revised edition. London: Constable.

Hinds, Manuel (1990) Issues in the introduction of market forces in Eastern European socialist economies. World Bank Internal Discussion Paper no. 0057, Washington, DC.

Hofman, Bert and Koop, Michael J. (1990a) Makroökonomische Aspekte der Reformen in Osteuropa. *Die Weltwirtschaft*, H. I, 161–72.

—— and —— (1990b) Monetary overhang and the dynamics of prices, exchange rates, and income in the transition to a market economy. Kiel Institute of World Economics, Kiel Discussion Paper no. 418.

IMF (1990) *The Economy of the USSR: Summary and Recommendations*. Washington, DC: IMF.

Institute of International Finance (1990) *Building Free Market Economies in Central and Eastern Europe: Challenges and Realities*. Washington, DC: IIF.

Kadar, Bela (1989) Comment on Jan Winiecki 'Eastern Europe: challenge of

1992 dwarfed by pressures of system's decline. In Horst Siebert (ed.), *The Completion of the Internal Market, Symposium.* Tübingen: J.C.B. Mohr (Paul Siebeck).

Kantzenbach, E. (1990) Ökonomische Probleme der deutschen Vereinigung: Anmerkungen zur jüngsten Wirtschaftsgeschichte. *Hamburger Jahrbuch für Wirtschafts- und Gesellschaftspolitik,* 35, 307–26.

Klodt, H., Schmidt, K.D. et al (1989) *Weltwirtschaftlicher Strukturwandel und Standortwettbewerb,* Kiel Institute of World Economics, Kieler Studien, Tübingen: J.C.B. Mohr (Paul Siebeck).

Kloten, Norbert (1990) Zur Transformation von Wirtschaftssystemen. *Ordo,* 40, 99–127.

Kluson, Vaclav (1990a) *Institutional Aspects of Privatization.* Prague: Czechoslovak Academy of Sciences, Institute of Economics (unpublished).

—— (1990b) *Zur Strategie der Privatisierung.* Prague: Czechoslovak Academy of Sciences, Institute of Economics.

Koop, Michael and Schmieding, H. (1991) Privatisierung in Mittel- und Osteuropa: Konzepte für den Hindernislauf zur Marktwirtschaft. Kiel Institute of World Economics, Kiel Discussion Paper no. 165.

Kornai, Janos (1980) *Economics of Shortage.* Amsterdam: North Holland.

—— (1990) *The Road to a Free Economy. Shifting from a Socialist System: the Example of Hungary.* New York: Norton.

Kostrzewa, Wojciech, Nunnenkamp, Peter and Schmieding, Holger (1989) A Marshall Plan for Middle and Eastern Europe? Kiel Institute of World Economics, Kiel Working Paper no. 403.

Lal, Deepak (1984) The political economy of the predatory state. World Bank, Development Research Department, Discussion Paper no. 105, Washington, DC.

—— (1987) The political economy of economic liberalization. *World Bank Economic Review,* 1 (2), 273–99.

—— (1990) The fable of the three envelopes: the analysis and political economy of the reform of Chinese state owned enterprises. *European Economic Review,* 34 (6), 1213–31.

Lammers, Konrad (1990) Mehr regionale Kompetenzen für die EG im Europäischen Binnenmarkt? Kiel Institute of World Economics, Kiel Working Paper no. 439.

Langhammer, Rolf J. and Nunnenkamp, Peter (1990) Country report Hungary. Kiel Institute of World Economics (mimeo).

Lehment, Harmen (1990) *Internationale Auswirkungen der deutschen Währungs-, Wirtschafts- und Sozialunion.* Würzburg: Verein für Sozialpolitik.

Lipton, David and Sachs, Jeffrey (1990) Creating a market economy in Eastern Europe: the case of Poland. *Brookings Papers on Economic Activity,* no. 1, 75–147.

Long, Ngo Van and Siebert, Horst (1991) Institutional competition versus ex-ante harmonization: the case of environmental policy. *Journal of Institutional and Theoretical Economics*, in the press.

McKinnon, Ronald I. (1981) Financial repression and the liberalization problem within less-developed countries. In Sven Grassman and Eric Lundberg (eds), *The World Economic Order: Past and Prospect*. New York: St Martin's Press, 365–86.

McClure, Charles E. Jr (1983) *Tax Assignment in Federal Countries*. Canberra: Australian National University, Centre for Research on Federal Financial Relations.

—— (1986) Tax competition: is what's good for the private goose also good for the public gander? *National Tax Journal*, 39, 341–8.

Messerlin, Patrick A. (1989) The EC antidumping regulations: a first economic appraisal, 1980–85. *Weltwirtschaftliches Archiv*, 125, no. 3.

Mohr, Ernst (1990) Environmental taxes and charges and EC fiscal harmonisation: theory and policy. Kiel Institute of World Economics, Kiel Discussion Paper no. 161.

Neumann, Manfred (1990) *Internationale Wirtschaftspolitik: Koordination, Kooperation oder Konflikt?* Würzburg: Verein für Socialpolitik.

Newbery, David M. (1991) Reform in Hungary: sequencing and privatization. *European Economic Review*, in the press.

Oates, Wallace E. and Schwab, Robert (1988) Economic Competition among jurisdictions: efficiency enhancing or distortion inducing? *Journal of Public Economics*, 35, 333–54.

Obstfeld, Maurice (1986) Capital mobility in the world economy: theory and measurement. *Carnegie-Rochester Conference Series on Public Policy*, 24, 55–104.

Ohmae, Kenichi (1985) *Triad Power. The Coming Shape of Global Competition*. London: Collier Macmillan.

Olson, Mancur (1969) The principle of 'fiscal equivalence'. The division of responsibilities among different levels of government. *American Economic Review*, 59, 479–87.

Paqué, Karl-Heinz (1989) Die soziale Dimension des EG-Binnenmarktes – Theorie, Bestandsaufnahme und Kritik. *Die Weltwirtschaft*, H. I, 112–23.

Pelkmans, Jacques L.M. (1984) *Market Integration in the European Community*. Den Haag.

PlanEcon (various) *PlanEcon Report. Developments in the Economies of the Soviet Union and Eastern Europe*. Washington DC: PlanEcon Inc.

Popper, Karl (1944) *The Open Society and Its Enemies*. London: Routledge.

Pratten, Cliff (1987) *The Management of Operating Business by Large Companies*. Aldershot: Gower.

—— (1988) A survey of the economies of scale. Internal Paper, Economic

Papers, Commission of the European Communities, no. 67, October, Brussels.

Prosi, Gerhard (1990) Comment on Horst Siebert: The harmonization issue in Europe: prior agreement or a competitive process. In Horst Siebert (ed.), *The Completion of the Internal Market*. Tübingen: J.C.B. Mohr (Paul Siebeck), 76–84.

Rodrik, Dani (1989) Liberalization, sustainability and the design of structural adjustment programs. Harvard University, J.F. Kennedy School, Working Paper no. 177 D.

—— (1990) How should structural adjustment programs be designed? *World Development*, 18 (7), 933–47.

Schmidt, Klaus-Dieter (1990) Die Renaissance des Kleinbetriebs. *Aspekte der Finanzierung des Kleinbetriebssektors, Betriebswirtschaftliche Schriften*, 131, 11–22.

Schmieding, Holger (1990) Der Übergang zur Marktwirtschaft: Gemeinsamkeiten und Unterschiede zwischen Westdeutschland 1948 und Mittel- und Osteuropa heute. *Die Weltwirtschaft*, H. I, 149–60.

Schumpeter, Joseph A. (1934) *The Theory of Economic Development. An Inquiry into Profits, Capital, Credit, Interest, and the Business Cycle*. Cambridge, MA: Harvard University Press.

Siebert, Horst (1985) Spatial aspects of environmental economics. In A.V. Kneese and J.L. Sweeney (eds), *Handbook of Natural Resource and Energy Economics, Vol. 1*. Amsterdam: North Holland, 125–64.

—— (1987) *Economics of the Environment*, 2nd edn. Berlin, Heidelberg, New York: Springer-Verlag.

—— (1989a) Europe '92. Environmental policy in an integrated market. Kiel Institute of World Economics, Kiel Working Paper no. 365.

—— (1989b) The harmonization issue in Europe: prior agreement or a competitive process. In Horst Siebert (ed.), *The Completion of the Internal Market*. Tübingen: J.C.B. Mohr (Paul Siebeck), 53–75.

—— (1989c) Perspektiven zur Vollendung des Europäischen Binnenmarktes. *Kyklos*, 4, 181–201.

—— (1989d) Harmonisierung der Mehrwertsteuer oder Anpassung der Wechselkurse. Kiel Institute of World Economics, Kiel Discussion Paper no. 156.

—— (1990a) Umweltpolitik in der Europäischen Gemeinschaft. Zentralisierung oder Dezentralisierung. Kiel Institute of World Economics, Kiel Working Paper no. 429.

—— (1990b) Locational competition in a Tiebout World. Comment on Vito Tanzi and Lans Bovenberg: is there a need for harmonizing capital income taxes within EC countries? In Horst Siebert (ed.), *Reforming Capital Income Taxation*, Tübingen: J.C.B. Mohr (Paul Siebeck), 206–8.

—— (1990c) The economic integration of Germany: an update. Kiel Institute of World Economics, Kiel Discussion Paper no. 160a.

—— (1990d) Prinzipien des deutschen Wirtschaftssystems. Kiel Institute of World Economics, Kiel Working Paper no. 445.

—— (1991a) The integration of Germany – real economic adjustment. *European Economic Review*, in the press.

—— (1991b) German economic union: the economics of transition. *Economic Policy*, in the press.

—— and Koop, Michael J. (1990) Institutional Competition. A concept for Europe? *Aussenwirtschaft*, 45 (IV), 439–62.

—— and Schmieding, Holger (1991) Restructuring industry in Eastern Germany. In Karel Cool et al. (eds), *European Industrial Restructuring in the 1990s*. London: Macmillan.

Sinn, Hans-Werner (1990a) Tax harmonization and tax competition in Europe. NBER Working Paper no. 3248, Cambridge, MA.

—— (1990b) Die Grenzen des Standortwettbewerbs. Lecture held at Vienna University, mimeo.

—— (1990c) Macroeconomic aspects of German unification. *Münchner Wirtschaftswissenschaftliche Beiträge*, no. 90–31.

Sinn, Stefan (1989a) Economic models of policy-making in interdependent economies: an alternative view on competition among policies. Kiel Institute of World Economics, Kiel Working Paper no. 390.

—— (1989b) Internationale Wettbewerbsfähigkeit von immobilen Faktoren im Standortwettbewerb. Kiel Institute of World Economics, Kiel Working Paper no. 361.

—— (1990) The taming of Leviathan: competition among governments. Kiel Institute of World Economics, Kiel Working Paper no. 433.

Soltwedel, Rüdiger (1987) Wettbewerb zwischen Regionen statt zentral koordinierter Regionalpolitik. *Die Weltwirtschaft*, H. I, 129–45.

Stat. Bundesamt (1990) *Jahrbuch der Bundesrepublik Deutschland für das Ausland*. Stuttgart.

Straubhaar, Thomas (1988) International labour migration within a common market: some aspects of EC experience. *Journal of Common Market Studies*, 27 (1), 45–62.

Summers, Robert and Heston, Allan (1988) A new set of international comparisons of real product and price level estimates for 130 countries, 1950–1985. *Review of Income and Wealth*, 34, 1–25.

Tanzi, Vito and Bovenberg, Lans (1990) Is there a need for harmonizing capital income taxes within EC countries? In Horst Siebert (ed.), *Reforming Capital Income Taxation*. Tübingen: J.C.B. Mohr (Paul Siebeck).

Tiebout, Charles M. (1956) A pure theory of local expenditure. *Journal of Political Economy*, 64, 325–33.

Trapp, Peter (1989) The European single market – opportunity or fortress? Kiel Institute of World Economics, Kiel Working Paper no. 385.

United Nations (1989) *Monthly Bulletin of Statistics*, May. New York: UN.

United Nations Economic Commission for Europe (1990) *Economic Reform in the East: a Framework for Western Support*. Geneva: UN.

Vaubel, Roland (1978) Strategies for currency unification and the case for a European parallel currency. Kieler Studien no. 156, Tübingen.

—— (1983) Coordination or competition among national macro-economic policies? In Fritz Machlup, Gerhard Fels and Hubertus Müller-Groeling (eds), Reflection on a Troubled World Economy, Essays in Honor of Herbert Giersch. Basingstoke: Macmillan, 1–28.

Verborn, Harrie A.A. (1989) Social insurance and the free internal market. University of Amsterdam, mimeo.

Vickers, John and Yarrow, George (1988) *Privatization: an Economic Analysis*, 2nd edn. Cambridge, MA: MIT Press.

Wallich, H.C. (1955) *Triebkräfte des deutschen Wiederaufstiegs*. Frankfurt: Knapp.

Willgerodt, Hans (1975) Die gesellschaftliche Aneignung privater Leistungserfolge als Grundelement der wettbewerblichen Marktwirtschaft. In Heinz Sauermann and Ernst J. Mestmäcker (eds), *Wirtschaftsordnung und Staatsverfassung*. Tübingen: J.C.B. Mohr (Paul Siebeck), 687–705.

Winiecki, Jan (1989) Eastern Europe: challenge of 1992 dwarfed by pressures of system's decline. In Horst Siebert (ed.), *The Completion of the Internal Market*. Tübingen: J.C.B. Mohr (Paul Siebeck), 275–95.

—— (1990) What have we learned from the Polish transition programme in its first year? Adam Smith Research Centre, Occasional Paper no. 1, Warsaw.

Wissenschaftlicher Beirat beim Bundesministerium für Wirtschaft (1988), *Stellungnahme zum Weissbuch der EG-Kommission über den Binnenmarkt*, Bonn.

World Bank (1990a) *World Debt Tables 1989/1990*. Washington, DC: World Bank.

World Bank (1990b) *World Development Report, 1990*. Washington, DC: World Bank.

Wyplosz, Charles (1991) On the real exchange rate effect of German unification. *Weltwirtschaftliches Archiv*, 127, in the press.

Index